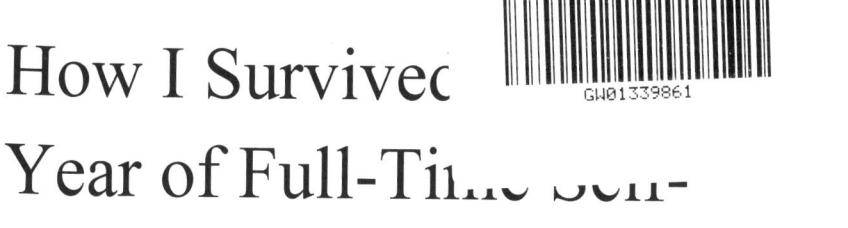

How I Survived [my First] Year of Full-Time Self-Employment: Going it Alone at 40

by

Liz Broomfield

© Liz Broomfield 2013. Not to be reproduced or sold without my permission.

Introduction

In 2009 I was offered the chance to proofread some student dissertations. I duly set myself up as self-employed (see the Appendices for how to do this), did the work, invoiced the customers and gathered in the payments. Fast forward to 2011: I was working part time at my day job and all sorts of hours at my proofreading. Oh, and editing, writing and transcribing, too. What had been a part-time job to earn some extra money and keep my brain cells working had turned into a very real promise of full-time self-employment.

When I looked around at materials and support for people like me, people who weren't traditional entrepreneurs, people who took it slowly and carefully, people who were administrators, lower-level employees with something extra to offer, I couldn't find much. At the same time, I was surprising myself with how passionate I was about sharing the message that you didn't need to BE Richard Branson, sell eggs to your school mates and jump in with a big load of debt in order to run your own business.

When it was time to go self-employed full time, I made two decisions. One was, erm, to go self-employed full time. The other was to blog my way through the process, at least for a year. I wasn't likely to change careers and switch lifestyles completely again; I was coming up for 40, and I wanted to keep a record of what happened, how I felt, and what I did as I went along.

I found that there are a lot of secrets in business – "Top 10 business secrets you must know", "Top 5 Marketing Ideas!" but not an awful lot of honesty and openness. So I shared exactly how I did it, the plans I made, how I knew when it was time to jump ship from the day job. As the year went on, I wrote articles on homeworkers' resolutions, on being an overnight success, on tax, on mutual support …

People enjoyed reading these articles, and other small business people, both those who are already established and those who were thinking of starting out, told me that they found the blog useful.

So as I came to the end of the year, I decided to weave these articles together with a diary of my first year of full-time self-employment. I've added in some extras at the end, all about working as a freelancer, and how to choose your freelance career.

I hope you find this book useful. The process of writing it has itself been very interesting to me. There is bonus material that you won't find on my blog, and I hope that my journey will inspire others to do it the safe and calm way!

Do let me know what you think of this book at liz@libroediting.com.

Acknowledgements

Major thanks go to Matthew for all the support, buns, cups of tea and dinners cooked. And to my friends for accepting that I wasn't around as much as I used to be, for telling their friends about my business, and for being behind me all the way.

Special thanks for making this year a lot easier go to Karen Strunks for organising the marvellous Social Media Café networking events which I go to every month to chat with peers; Coral Musgrave for services to sharing and retweeting; Podnosh for enabling my (and others') "giving something back" by running the Social Media Surgeries; Adam Yosef for taking the best pictures of me and helping me project a professional image; Katharine O'Moore-Klopf for being an inspirational freelance editor and supportive friend; Linda Bates for taking on jobs at the last minute; Sian Edwards for introducing me to an important source of jobs (and for being round the corner working from home too); my lovely clients for sending me their projects (and paying their invoices); LA Fitness and Marvin Edinborough for keeping me fit and sane; my Twitter and Facebook business friends for sharing my posts and supporting me; local self-employed friends for all the coffee and chat.

Special book-related thanks to my marvellous beta readers and editors, Chrys Schlapak and Catherine Fitzsimons: you made my book much better, and all remaining errors are of course my own.

Contents

Introduction iii
Acknowledgements v
Contents..vii
Before..9
   Setting the scene and setting the boundaries...............9
   A typical week – before...10
   Leaving the safe haven of employment........................15
   Diary Entry: My first week of self-employment..........17
January 21
   Unexpected free time 21
   Exactly how I did it..22
   *Diary Entry 29 Jan: Officially full-time self-employed*26
February 31
   Tee hee 31
   How to be an overnight business success...................33
   Diary Entry 28 February: Keep calm and carry on? .36
   How to relieve the pressure 39
March..41
   Keeping calm and carrying on 41
   A typical week of full-time self-employment 44
   On (not) taking risks 48
April 51
   End of year...51
   Why I do my tax in April 53
   Diary Entry 12 April: Working out my tax 56
May...59
   Is the stress worth it? 59
   Diary Entry 18 May: Home alone 62
   *Good things about working from home in the summer*63
June..65
   On bank holidays 65
   A typical day for Libro..66
   On presenteeism..68
July...71
   Diary Entry 02 July: The first six months...................71
   On mutual support 75
   Paper is sometimes best! 76

August 79
   Diary Entry 01 Aug: Happy Birthday, Libro! *79*
   Looking at your statistics *80*
   Diary Entry 31 Aug: A holiday from WiFi! *85*
September 87
   On social media and networking *87*
   Diary Entry 17 Sep: Back to school *90*
October 93
   But how can I be ill? *93*
   On getting slummocky *95*
November 99
   How are you motivated? *99*
   What the well-dressed homeworker is wearing *103*
   Diary Entry 20 Nov: Give me a break! *110*
December 113
   The holy grail of passive income *113*
   The first day of the second year *116*
   Where now for Libro? *117*
   Rounding off the year: an interview with myself *121*
April 2013 123
   A mature business *123*
Conclusion 125
Appendix 1: So you want to be a freelancer? 127
Appendix 2: How to go about being self-employed . 131
Appendix 3: A Homeworker's Resolutions 134
Appendix 4: Tips for Working with Clients 137
Appendix 5: Tips for Working with Freelancers 141
Appendix 6: Setting Goals 145
Appendix 7: Resource guide 148

Before

Setting the scene and setting the boundaries

I started my business, Libro, in August 2009. I'd been doing bits and pieces of editing for people on an unpaid basis for years, and had lots of experience in various jobs, but it was when a colleague at the Library where I worked (full-time at the time) asked me if I could proofread a couple of students' dissertations that I decided to go for it, set up the company, registered with the Inland Revenue and went on an HMRC course to find out what to do.

My roster of clients grew, and rather than work every hour of the day on both the day job and the business, I decided to go part time at the Library, dropping one day a week in January 2011 and a further day in May. I kept spreadsheets of how I was doing against my targets, built up my customer base gradually, diversified to offer proofreading, copyediting, writing, typing, transcription and localisation, and I could see during November 2011 that it was time to make the big move and take the business full time from January.

My regular customers by this point included a few I'd picked up in 2010, including a tender-writing company and a journalist who needed interviews to be transcribed; and more and more collected in 2011, including a student proofreading agency, some graduate students, companies in Poland, China, India and Finland that used my proofreading services for materials translated into English but needing that extra polish, and a successful author who started off using my transcription services then booked me to edit her religious thriller. At the end of 2011 I picked up a big transcription client that took me safely through my first year of self-employment, and as we will see, I kept gaining new regular clients throughout 2012.

Some boundary setting: I won't be talking about my clients by name or by identifiable features (so, if I've worked for you, don't worry if you're reading this).

A typical week – before

I thought it might be useful to write down what happened in a typical work week when I was part-time employed and part-time self-employed, just before going full-time with Libro. The work level had a horrible habit of building to a peak just before I dropped some Library hours, then had a terrifying slump directly afterwards. Anyway, this is a typical week of part-time employment and part-time self-employment:

A quick key before we start:

Blog posts – I had two blogs at this point, my professional and language one at www.libroediting.com and my new self-employment blog starting up at www.librofulltime.wordpress.com.

Editing – Making a text work in terms of grammar, punctuation, spelling, word choice, sentence structure, etc.

Proofreading – Really this is making sure a document is ready for publication, but especially my student clients tend to use this term interchangeably with "editing".

Transcription – Used to be called audio-typing: basically turning words on a tape into words in a document

Localisation – Changing the spellings, grammar, word choices and idioms of a text in American English to make it suitable for a British English audience

Although this diary is soaked in these terms, if you're not an editor, what you'll get out of it is what it was: busy, busy, busy!

Monday 28 November – I posted a blog post on my language and business blog – handily, I'd managed to write up a few posts in advance so could just publish them as I went this week. I worked 7.45-3.50 at the Library. Rushed out of the house as soon as I got back with some post as I needed to wait in for a parcel for M on Tuesday. Came home and did two hours' transcribing and some other bits and bobs. Watched a silly TV programme for light relief.

Tuesday 29 November – a Libro Day. Did another hour of transcribing; spent two hours editing a dissertation (it was a pdf, I have special software for these but, even though the English was good, it took me longer than if it had been in Word); spent over three hours editing a paper for a journal (including ensuring the bibliography was as the journal requires: this was actually the most time-consuming part); did some bits for a translator I work for. I also did some admin – writing and responding to emails, requests for quotations, etc. I had a proper lunch (hooray) but didn't get out of the house until after dark, when I met M in Sainsburys to get some bits and bobs. I try to get out of the house during daylight, but this wasn't possible today!

Wednesday 30 November – another Libro Day. Published a blog post about emotions in business that I'd been inspired to write last week. Finished off the transcription I was doing in 1 hour 45 mins including spell-checking (a two-person Webinar for a lovely client – the topic is interesting to me, which does help, although I will transcribe just about anything!). I edited another article for yesterday's client, but a shorter one this time that only took a couple of hours and did a localisation into British English for another regular – this time a website for an international company. In addition to all this I found time to do an hour or so of cleaning, cook a batch of meals so I have a quicker dinner time in the week, and go for a short run (in the daylight!). Before dinner, I got most of my monthly invoicing done – most of my regular clients are sent one invoice a month for all the work I have done for them during that month. What I didn't do was go to the Birmingham Entrepreneurs Meetup, a monthly event in town that I do enjoy. But I just didn't have the time and had to send my apologies.

Thursday 1 December – a Library day so worked 7.45-3.50 again. I wrote my first post for my new blog at lunch time after deciding to launch it during the morning! Came home and recorded the payments that had already come in from yesterday's invoicing (I like the beginning of the month). I went through the document one of my coaching clients had sent me for half an hour (I am helping them to get down to writing up their thesis) and replied to a request for a quotation. Then I stopped for the evening and went for a run with M before dinner. After dinner, some frantic BookCrossing admin (a hobby I used to spend a lot of time on!) then some relaxation time, watching a bit of telly.

Friday 2 December – woke up early and sorted out some more books, then lugged them into the Library to stock the BookCrossing Zone I set up here. A colleague took over running the Zone a few months ago, but I like to keep it filled up when I can. I published a prepared Troublesome Pairs blog post. A normal day at the Library, worked till 3.50 then home for some Libro bits and pieces ... I logged in to an admin site to upload a business feature onto a client's local business pages (he'd called me on the Libro mobile to ask me to do it this morning but I'd left the phone at home – this is one of the stressful things about my double life) and finished off negotiations on a piece of work for the weekend, polishing some translated English. I took delivery of some boxes of business directories for my local Business Association – I joined a few months ago, will be on the Committee from January, and M has kindly offered to help me put them through letterboxes tomorrow (my friend at work suggested that this might be so he could actually spend some time with me: I fear she's right!). Off to the gym to get some exercise in and see a friend who goes on a Friday evening and then relaxed for the rest of the evening. This is actually proving to be quite a light week, but you can see I'm still doing something for Libro every day ...

Saturday 3 December – I did a bit of housekeeping before breakfast, putting together, publishing and publicising my weekly "Freelancer/Small Business Chat" feature on the blog. Then I had a bit of a read in bed – a rare luxury – before we got ourselves together for the day and spent two hours delivering the local Business Association directory to 480 addresses on our road and surrounding side streets. Harder work than I thought – lots of exercise opening gates, running up paths and pushing the book through all sorts of letterboxes! After a late lunch, bought at the Farmers' Market, I put in a couple of hours working on a translation from an Eastern European language into English – my job was to polish it to make it look like it was written by a native British English speaker. I then spent 30 minutes or so working on a few blog posts for friends who I skill swap with on an irregular basis. I recorded another payment from a regular client in my spreadsheet, noting that I'd hit the first of my range of 4 income targets for the month (this one was "replace the money from the 2 days I didn't work at the library") and then I was free for dinner, a bit of BookCrossing admin, etc.

Sunday 4 December – a billable-hours free day, I managed to work in my usual Sunday pastimes of a run in the morning, and a visit to the local cafe with a friend in the afternoon. I almost always get the run in; sometimes Libro stops me going to the cafe, mainly because I know I'll be at the day job on Monday. I put in a couple of hours writing blog posts in the afternoon; I like to get ahead of myself, but I didn't have one written for Monday and I needed to put together a guest post I'm publishing in the week. I also wrote my newsletter as I've realised the next edition is due this week. I also, excitingly, wrote an abstract to submit to the Iris Murdoch Society to see if they'll invite me to contribute a presentation to the IM Conference in September 2012. Something I really need to do once I'm full-time with Libro is give some time to my research project and I hadn't really found time to get this done!

Summary – so, actually this wasn't a hugely, horribly, frantically busy Libro week like some have been. I did 14 hours of billable Libro work (covering my billable work target) but of course I also did a significant number of hours on admin, including monthly invoicing and writing. So it's more like 18 or so hours if you add those in. Plus the 21 hours at the library. Plus two hours delivering those directories … In the weeks previous to this one I've done 23, 20, 16 and 18 hours on Libro, which makes it a lot more difficult. But there you have it – a week in the life "before" …

Just to break those work/work days down a bit more, on a day when I worked in the office and at home, my day would look like this:

5.45 – 6.00 Get up, check Libro email, maybe do some Libro work

6.00 – 7.00 Breakfast, shower, get ready for work.

7.00 – 7.30 Travel into work.

7.30 – 13.00 Working at the Library.

13.00 – 13.30 Lunch. Check Blackberry and reply to Libro emails / make calls.

13.30 – 15.45 Working at the Library.

15.45 – 16.30 Travelling home.

16.30 – 19.30 Cup of tea then working till M gets home and beyond. He makes my dinner.

19.30 – 20.00 Hasty dinner.

20.00 – 22.30 Working on Libro projects.

22.30 – 23.00 Getting ready for bed.

23.00 Bedtime.

That was 4 then 3 days a week through the whole of 2011 pretty well. Phew! Then there would be 1 or 2 weekdays a week just on Libro and working solidly on Libro at the weekends. Not so much gym, certainly not any cafe with friends, not so many blog posts, not so much reading!

Leaving the safe haven of employment: An emotional day

I had a bit of an odd time in mid-December. At the library, there was a lot of passing knowledge on, and quite a few "last things" – I did my last lot of monthly statistics for the department (and talked my manager through my notes on it), which seems like a small thing, but I took the task on well over a year previously, spent ages streamlining it so I didn't have to type stuff in twice, etc., and it was more of a complex task, maybe, than other run of the mill things. I had been training another colleague on a lot of bits and bobs and seeing the work going to her rather than me – again, a natural thing, but there was a little connection lost each time and I floated a little freer each time it happened.

I said goodbye to a few colleagues who wouldn't be in for my last day. With one, it was OK, as I know I'll keep in touch and we'll see each other again. With another, it was harder – I've worked with her for years and years, including a good few months where it was just us two in the same office three days a week; she's so lovely and I miss her, but I didn't really see that we'll be in touch so much. I did choke back a tear as I said goodbye.

I had a few presents – which I really wasn't expecting – two from office-mates and one from the ladies who run the charity that I've supported through my running and other endeavours. I opened cards but not presents, as I was expecting to have an emotional – if not physical – hangover on Tuesday and thought it would be nice to have something to look forward to.

I had a few afternoons off in that last week so I could balance out the flexitime I'd accrued, so a lot of travelling home alone at odd times, a bit sad and wistful: I had a load of Libro work to do, and Christmas cards to write if I ran out of that: but I did feel sad, and I acknowledged that as a rational reaction to the week, and pressed on.

And so it came to my last day. Although I would still be getting up early to start work every morning, I knew I wouldn't particularly miss the dark, cold walk up my road to the main road to catch the bus! Of course it wasn't always dark when I went out, but it had been these past few December weeks. The campus wasn't quite as dark when I came in, but near enough. The library looked atmospheric and cosy with its lights on. As dawn comes up, all of the trees filled with birds, twittering away. I knew I would miss working on such a lovely site.

Jennifer, my dear desk-mate, took some photos of me at my desk … and I took one of her with my view up the office from my corner desk. I also took one of the view out of our window. I could watch the seasons change on the trees outside. At least we could see outside – in two of the offices I worked in before, I couldn't see the sky at all!

A few people from the office joined me for lunch. My manager passed on a card and presents with no fuss, which is exactly how I wanted it to be. As we walked back, the sun went in a bit, which was a shame, as the campus had been looking just as it did in 1988 when I first visited on an Open Day.

After I'd finished work I went across to Staff House. The coffee bar wasn't open so I sat on a sofa in the foyer with my hot cross bun and current read. Friends gradually came and joined me and then a lovely number of colleagues – M's as well as my own - came by to wish me good luck and have a drink. M and I went for a curry with a couple of the others ... and had a bit of a late one! The next morning, I opened my gifts from my friends and emailed to thank them.

And then, the next day, once I'd opened my presents, it was Libro all the way, with a vengeance, with four projects to complete from my regulars, a quotation in for another larger project and some student work coming over. No time to be maudlin, as it turned out!

Diary Entry 16 December 2012: My first week of self-employment

I had my leaving do on Monday and it was go, go, go from then on! Before that last weekend, I just had one transcription booked in for this week, coming in on Thursday. "Fine," I thought, "I can get my Christmas cards and the cleaning done, and have a bit of a rest". Well, it wasn't quite to be like that.

I had an enquiry about a job while I was actually at my leaving do. Thank goodness for the BlackBerry and the fact that I'm almost teetotal! I sent a holding message with details of my availability and pricing, and negotiated that job the next morning, copyediting/proofreading part of a professional rulebook (I was both checking the spelling, etc., and comparing it to last year's book to make sure that no differences had crept in): I got the job right away.

I had an edition of the club magazine I've been editing for nearly two years in on Monday night, too, plus some pieces from a student proofreading company I work with and a feature to write from a regular. So that all got done on Tuesday. On Wednesday I finished the big project and did a little bit for a new client. I managed a trip to the gym and I had a Christmas meal with my friends from BookCrossing. I didn't know how much BookCrossing would remain a part of my life, but I did want (badly) to spend more time with my friends. On Thursday, having still not written my Christmas cards or done the cleaning, I did more student work, polished a translation from the Polish, did an hour or so of copyediting for another regular, and popped into town to have a meeting with a potential new client about writing a set of blog posts for them. When I got home, I wrote out my Christmas cards and went for a chilly run.

On Friday, I emailed notes from our meeting to the potential new client, looked at a chapter of a PhD for a client whose other chapters I worked on last week, did some more student work, posted my Christmas cards, AND did the cleaning! Hooray! On Saturday we had a family lunch and then a party at M's bosses' house to go to: I transcribed for one of my regular transcription clients and did some student work in the morning before I went out. I got home to a message from the new client that they would like to accept my price and service offer and asking for my invoice for their deposit. And on Saturday I finished that transcription and did a bit more copyediting, around going to the gym and watching the Strictly Come Dancing final on catch-up in the morning and visiting a friend in the evening, with a crisp and icy walk home. I also emailed my regulars to tell them about a commitment I had early next year (Jury Service – bad timing!) which might affect response times for a little while.

I had two transcriptions to do for my journalist client and a web page to copyedit for the next week, plus doing final edits and some reference checking on a non-fiction book I'd been working on for a while. I had a novel and a PhD due in, too. I did promise to have Christmas Day off [and I did]!

I wrote out a list of New Job Resolutions, mainly around going outside in the daylight and having proper lunches, and I achieved both those things all week. I also managed to keep warm!

I did 29 hours 15 mins of billable work this week, beating my targets, and have brought in almost my target for the month in incoming payments, so I'm really pleased about that. I know every week wouldn't be this good, but it has been a good one to have, to help with the transition into full-time Libro.

However, although in my head I understand that I am now with Libro, I have to support myself, etc., etc., I realise that I haven't really come to terms with it yet. It sort of feels like I'm on annual leave from the library job and will be going back there afterwards, and I suspect it might only hit me after the New Year …

January

January was a month where I got used to working for myself full time (once I'd negotiated that bout of badly-timed Jury Service) and started to revel in the freedom. Time to reflect would come later: it was all so exciting! But I did take the time to note down exactly how I did it. But first, something unexpected …

Unexpected free time

What do you do with sudden, unexpected free time?

I was sent home from Jury Service at lunchtime on my first Wednesday and told not to come back until the next Monday. Now, because I knew they were free in advance, Thursday and Friday didn't seem to count as "unexpected" free time. But that afternoon did, very much so: it felt like a delicious, almost wicked treat.

I have to admit that my first impulse was to get some things done which had been pushed back. So I designed and ordered some business cards for Libro, and took the opportunity to write up some blog posts in advance so I could have the luxury of just hitting the "publish" button the next week when I was back at the Court.

But I also carved out the small luxury of being curled up on the sofa, with my book, when M came home. There was a – large – cup of tea in there too, of course. And I got through loads of the book, making it another (oh, joy!) book that I didn't take weeks to finish.

Exactly how I did it

I'm still glad that I soft-launched Libro in the way I did, first working at the Library full-time (August 2009 – December 2010), then part-time (January – April 2011), then even more part-time (May – December 2011).

I managed to save up enough money to support myself for a year while I was full time, and I lived on my reduced wages, more or less, during 2011. This meant that I could already cover living expenses for 2012, and only needed to make a year's living money out of Libro's earnings for 2011-12 and 2012-13 in order to survive the year after that, reducing the stress and expectations.

The slow build-up meant that I knew I could do it – much less risk for me, again.

Being already experienced running Libro while having that safety net meant that I was already aware of the ups and downs. If an invoice went unpaid for a little longer than I'd like, I didn't have to be all "OMG: penury!!" about it – I could just draw on past experience to wait for (or push for) the money.

If things appeared tedious, tiring or stressful, that's nothing to working 8 hours in one job, coming home and getting my head down to another 4 at the other one. Or working late for Libro and having to get up early to finish something before going in to the University.

I built up a support network and cheerleaders amongst ex-colleagues and other people I met along the way – so I continue to have a peer group for editing or small business matters, and a group of local friends who I can go to for non-work related gossip and chat or support.

I was able to identify the networking groups that are truly valuable: if they were worth taking time off a paid job for, they are worth continuing to attend now.

It was worth doing this so that it wasn't so scary to jump ship when it became time to do so.

So, how exactly did I make the transition from part-time "pin money" business to full-time business that is able to support me? At the time I wasn't even sure that it would work: looking back I can see of course that it did. The back-up information and statistics that made this clear to me are easy for you to replicate:

I kept records – right from the start (and thanks in large part to the HMRC course I attended just after I set myself up) I kept records of my invoices and outgoings on a spreadsheet. I always recorded both my monthly income and my full annual incomings and outgoings (based on the UK April-March financial year, which is Libro's financial year too). I still do this, and it means that at any one point in time I can see:

* Which invoices are still outstanding
* My income for this month (and previous months)
* My income, outgoings and profit for the current financial year, as of today

It was quite easy to do this, using fairly simple Excel skills, with the main invoices sheet feeding information into the other sheets as I go along (no retyping: no room for error)

I've had goals – I'll admit: when I started Libro I had no idea that I was ever going to take it full-time. But as I realised that I was working more hours on the two jobs than I really wanted to, I set goals for myself, so I could see when I would be able to drop a day at the day job in favour of Libro. This is how I did it:

I worked out how much money I would lose per month if I dropped a day at the library. To do this, I divided my monthly gross salary by 5. So to move to 4 days a week and replace the lost income, Libro would have to earn 1/5 of my monthly library salary per month.

I added a column to my monthly income spreadsheet called "Against 1/5 target". The amount in that cell for each month was my 1/5 salary minus my Libro earnings for that month. So if the amount needed to replace my salary was £400 and I earned £350, then I had brought in -£50 against target. Or was £50 under target.

I made this into a graph – a great way to see immediately where I was against target!

I added a cumulative target too – this meant that if I made £350 one month and £450 the next, my records would iron out the ups and downs to show if I was covering targets on average.

Once the 1/5 target was being achieved every month for 6 months, I knew it was time to negotiate dropping a day at the library and did so, starting the new regime in January 2011.

Then I repeated, using a 2/5 target, and used this to show me that I could drop a second day in May 2011. Which I did.

5/5 i.e. total salary replacement was my next target. But targets should be SMART (specific, measurable, achievable, realistic and time-based) and that was a bit scary at that point, and seemed too far away. So I sorted out some interstitial targets of 3/5 and 4/5 salary replacement. In fact, I cheated slightly – because I was managing to live on 3/5 of my salary at that point, I adjusted these last 3 to be a bit lower, giving me a lower target to replace, knowing I could live on that lower amount.

I saved up – Once I realised that I was likely to want to move to a more part-time basis with my job, I saved and saved and saved. It helps that interest rates are so low, oddly enough: I was happier to sacrifice my savings to living expenses, knowing that they wouldn't do much in a savings account. But I made sure that I had a whole year of living expenses saved up before I left my job, so 2012 was covered.

I cut costs – By hoarding Amazon vouchers for when I had to have new books, using BookCrossing and charity shops as other sources of books, not buying new clothes, etc., etc. – all very boring stuff but vital – I managed to live off my reduced wages from the Library through my part-time year. This meant that all my earnings from 2011 and 2012 could go to paying my way in 2013.

I worked hard - Because I always needed to be working enough to replace my salary for a good few months before I dropped the day in question, in three periods in my Libro life (Oct-Nov 2010, Mar-Apr 2011 and Sep-Nov 2011) I was working rather too many hours in the 2 combined jobs to be entirely comfortable. But I'd rather have it this way than leave myself vulnerable. It was hard to do 7.5 hours at the library, come home and do 3-4 more some evenings, and maybe 5 each day at the weekend. But no one got anywhere without working hard.

I made sacrifices (and so did other people – sorry!) – I had to prioritise Libro. So I had to postpone or cancel meeting up with friends; accepted that I couldn't keep up with my Twitter and Facebook timelines; didn't spend as much time with my Other Half as I would have wished and certainly didn't go on trips out with him; practically gave up reading for pleasure; didn't spend out on anything unnecessary ... but you don't get anywhere without some sacrifices, and I knew by a certain point that this would be temporary.

I was pretty darned blatant - I told everyone what I was doing. I cajoled and begged people into giving out my business cards, into retweeting my Tweets and sharing my Facebook posts. I started going to networking events – everything I could to do raise awareness of the business. I asked for references and testimonials, I asked for recommendations; I carried on marketing myself even when I was busy with work already.

I did all the other stuff I have written about regarding how to run your small business. I won't repeat that here. Pop to the Appendices if you want to see more.

I said it out loud – at one point this year I started announcing to all and sundry that I was aiming to leave the day job. I took advice, I asked for support, but I claimed it for myself. Powerful stuff, if a bit scary.

So there you go: that's how I did it. It's one way, it might not be the best way, but it worked for me.

Diary Entry 29 Jan: Officially full-time self-employed

January 22 ended my first proper full-time week with Libro. In December, although I worked just on Libro for the second part of the month, I was still employed by the University and being paid by them. The first two weeks of January were supposed to be my Jury Service weeks: in the end, I wasn't called for a case and only did four half days there, but I'd put off work (or done it in advance) so, certainly in the first week, I didn't have the usual amount to do. I had the rest that I should have had over Christmas, in fact. But these two weeks, it's just been me and Libro.

Work

I'm going to record a "typical week" later on in the year, just like I did when I was doing two jobs. I don't feel things have settled down enough yet to know what a typical week is, so I'll just summarise what I've got up to this week. I've edited articles for two regular clients and documents for one of those. I've proofread a PhD and some smaller academic pieces; the PhD was for a new direct client and the other pieces were for a student proofreading company who contract out work to me. I also edited a local history book and converted it into e-book format for the author, edited a downloadable document for another regular, and typed up a transcription of an interview for my journalist client. I did a bit of writing for my retail shelving client and another business listings client, a little bit of transcription, and a localisation using some software with which I was previously unfamiliar. I did an average of 32 billable hours per week, plus more hours doing admin and marketing, including responding to requests for price and service quotations. This means I've hit all my targets for income for January and my billable hours targets for each week (how much I earn, rather than how much comes in), which is handy for my goals (see Appendix 5).

Non-work activities

Or maybe I should call some of this non-billable-work activities! I've been to my first Jelly co-working event.[1] This is a monthly get-together organised by a local writer and event organiser, and I've been keen to attend for a while, but it falls on a day when I would normally have been working at the Library, and it never felt right to take too many days off for networking. This event takes place in the Jewellery Quarter, which is a bit of a walk across town, but in a cafe I know well, and we all sat around a big table, laptops out, working and chatting. The other attendees were a mixture of people I'd met before and new people, and it was a very nice, sociable occasion. I have to do most of my work in my quiet office, and I did plan to write up some blog posts, but ended up working on a client's thesis, which was perhaps the wrong project to choose. But I'd definitely go again

---

[1] http://www.yelp.co.uk/biz/birmingham-jelly-birmingham

I also went to Social Media Cafe[2] on Friday morning and had a lovely time catching up with business chums and meeting new people. I did do some work and there is a photo of me doing so, but it was fine to whip out the laptop, polish off a quick check of someone's English translation (I was charging by the word, not the hour: I wouldn't work in a public place if I was doing the latter), then close it and carry on networking. It was quite funny to think I was caught out working when I should be chatting, though! And I went to the BookCrossing meetup on Saturday, too.

Other activities included writing up some blog posts: I'm doing a series on how to use Word effectively, complete with screen prints, and I went through and created draft blog posts for all the Troublesome Pairs people had suggested (see the Libro blog[3] for all of these). I like to get ahead with blog posts so I can just publish them quickly when I'm busy with other work.

I also had the first Friday evening and most of Saturday off for my birthday. I had a lovely time and it was good to relax and see friends. I also had AN AFTERNOON OFF! I went away from my desk, away from my office, away from my house, away from my city … and had lunch and a book shopping expedition with a friend from America who was staying in Stratford. Yes, I did have to tell my regulars who send me urgent fast-turnaround work, and yes, I did have to work right up to the moment when I left the house, and check my BlackBerry on the way round, but I did have an afternoon off.

Apart from those social/networking occasions, I had a guest blog post published and was quoted in an article about the rise in numbers of self-employed people, spent a few hours delivering business

---

[2] http://birminghamsmc.com/
[3] http://www.libroediting.com/

directories for the local Business Association (I'm in the directory: v. exciting!) and even found time for a bit of work:

Looking forward, I have booked in to do some more transcription for a client I worked with just before Christmas, and I've got 2 new coaching clients, both doing Master's degrees, who I will be working with through to their dissertation submissions. So it's looking positive on the work front, and I've got some coffees and lunches with friends planned too.

Is this different from having two jobs?

One difference I noticed quite markedly this month was the effect a long day of Libro work had on my life and energy levels. On Wednesday, I had to get through proofreading most of a PhD thesis, plus some other bits and pieces. I ended up working an 11 1/2 hour day (I did get out, to the gym, for half an hour of rowing!). I worked late, and I was tired by the end of the day. But it was great to know that, if I needed to, I could rest on Thursday. Actually I ended up getting up early to complete a job I'd had to put off from the Wednesday, but just knowing I wasn't going to HAVE to get up at a particular time and get myself across to the office was great.

And ... this is going to sound a bit smug. But you know the Sunday Afternoon Blahs – the feeling you get when you know you have to go back to the office on Monday? Well, not only have I not had that for a couple of weeks; today I had the Sunday Morning Whoos, when I realised I wasn't going to have the Blahs this afternoon!

One disadvantage of leaving the day job

Some of my ex-colleagues came to my birthday dinner on Friday night. I hadn't seen them since my last day, and two of them live a little way away, which makes it hard to just meet up. I realised that I really miss them all – more than I maybe thought I would. Does that sound horrible? We all have colleagues we get on with, but we also all have people from old jobs where we've said, "Ooh, keep in touch, we must go out some time" … and then don't. Well, I want to see these people more, and I've already emailed them to say so!

In conclusion …

It's been a good couple of weeks. I've read more and seen my friends more. I've continued networking and marketing myself, and I've worked hard for my customers. Life is easier and more flexible – I'm certainly enjoying being able to go to the gym in the day time, when it's so much quieter. I have also hit the middle of my three monthly earning (that's money physically coming in to my account) targets already, and on aggregate, have hit my billable hours (money going onto invoices, but not always yet in) target per week. I hope this stays the same next week …

February

In February, I really started to settle in to my new lifestyle. Things became more automatic and comfortable, and although I don't think I really realised that I was self-employed, still feeling like I was on some kind of extended holiday from work, I began to see that it really was working. However, it then started to work a bit TOO well, and I had a bit of a crisis of confidence.

February was a good month on the regular customers front: I gained some new ones, including a translation agency based in Finland who started to send me work translated from Finnish into English to polish in British or American English, and, indeed, they are still regulars at the time of writing.

I wrote quite a few articles, some of which I'm going to share with you here, including one on that vital ingredient of the home worker's life: tea.

Tee hee

My name is Liz and I'm a tea-aholic. There: I've said it. And I don't mean to mock AA meetings, just to echo. I probably, in reality, do have a slight problem. I get tetchy if I don't have regular cuppas, and I have been known to develop a headache if I haven't had my first cup of the day early enough. In fact, when I was sorting out a logo for Libro, I nearly went for a tea-related image ... Anyway, although I'm not at the high level of tea expertise and variety achieved by my colleague Katharine O'Moore Klopf,[4] I do have a large selection of teas in the kitchen cabinet, and I've realised that I use different teas for different times, different moods, different kinds of work ...

---

[4] http://www.kokedit.com/ckb_teavendors.php

Earl Grey

The LyzzyBee standard. This is my red label or builder's tea. I start the day with a cup of Earl Grey, it's my tea of choice when out and about, and when I was working in an office and it seemed a bit silly to stock the whole range, this is what I stuck with. A cup with breakfast and yes, teabags do travel with me to foreign climes, just in case. I go for the Sainsburys Taste The Difference teabag in general, although I am given other brands and like them too. The Twinings one has apparently recently changed recipe, and there are some interesting variants, for example the lavender and jasmine ones. Stop press: I tried these and didn't take to them, and had to pass them on to another tea-drinking household!

Lady Grey

A Twinings tea and my favourite for during the day, standard variety. It's like the Earl, but with more citrus – refreshing on a warm day, cheery on a cold one.

Darjeeling

I bought this when I was looking for an alternative to the Lady Grey – it's another supermarket one, bought when I felt a bit guilty about spending out on tea (I don't any more). Although it is sold as being light and delicate, I find it more oomphy than Earl Grey, and so it's useful when I need more of a pick-me-up, or to be dragged through a difficult project.

Chai

For some unknown reason, I like to sip a Chai when I'm transcribing. Really, only then in a work context. Why? No idea! I drink it outside work, and tend to manage to avoid the compulsion to type out everything I hear, which is useful.

Spicy Tea

My friend Ali got me some Taylors of Harrogate Spicy Christmas Tea leaves the other year and I love it and will be sourcing more. Sometimes it's nice to go for the tea leaves – and I have a nifty in-cup strainer bought at Whittards so I don't need to crack out the teapot every time.

Lapsang Souchong

I really, really have to be in the mood for this smoky tea – but when I am I have to have gallons of the stuff. I don't think I've ever combined it with Libro work, though …

Peppermint, spearmint and green tea with jasmine

I have the odd flare-up of IBS and peppermint/ spearmint tea really soothe that. I had the green tea with jasmine in my library office drawer and had forgotten about it. It is, like all jasmine tea, oddly redolent of Savlon, but it is nice and calming. I might look at that for a mid-afternoon cuppa in future.

So there we go. Tea keeps me focused, it gives me exercise going down and up two flights of stairs every time I want a cuppa, and it keeps me hydrated and Libro running. What's your favourite work tea?

How to be an overnight business success

Someone posted on Twitter that people should follow me because I've built up my business so quickly. And yes, as I went full time I did hit the ground running at full capacity. But I don't feel like it's been an overnight success, and here's why (and why I think that's a good thing).

How have I brought myself up to full capacity since I went full time? It's been a combination of things:

- having a good set of regular customers I can rely on to keep sending me work

- having a marketing strategy which keeps people aware of what I do

- carefully using a few sources to help me gain more work

- keeping careful track of what I can and can't do, and being selective about what work I take on

These all mean that I could grow the business slowly while I was part time, and then ramp things up to fill in the full time hours.

Keeping regular

I built up a roster of regular customers over the early years – some who send me lots of work, some who send me something every now and again. I made sure to keep them happy, keeping them informed of when I was available when I worked part time, setting sensible expectations and being reliable. I also kept these diversified, from editing, to writing, to transcription. I let them know first when I went full time, I kept them as my priority customers, with others fitting around them – and they rewarded me by sending me more projects to work on.

Read all about it!

My Libro blog[5] was (and is) primarily written to be useful and helpful, of course. But my aim in starting it was also to drive business to my website. Do a quick Google search for "troublesome pairs", "spelled or spelt" and "what is a transcriber?" and you should find me on the first page of results. In early 2011, I instigated a

---

[5] http://libroediting.com/blog/

policy of making sure I got hits on the website every day, and often had to go and publicise myself on different fora to do so on a particular day. Now I have lots of hits every day, I never have to do that, and most of my hits come from search engines.

I also kept on networking and using social media. All of this ensured that I had a steady stream of new customers finding me and heading my way.

Paid help

I looked at a lot of freelancer websites when I started out – where you register and then bid for jobs. But I was never successful and I found that I was constantly underbid by companies offering the work for peanuts. Thanks to my friend, Sian, I found www.proz.com which is a site for translators. I took out a paid membership in 2011, which means that people who want editing, proofreading, transcribing and localisation services are given my details and can come through to me for a price and service estimate. Some really good, regular, clients have found me this way, with minimal effort from me (setting up my profile and then of course responding to questions and requests for quotations) and it was well worth choosing this one site to use. Getting a recommendation to use the site from someone else who had had success with it was key here.

There are lots of similar sites for whatever industry you might be in. Ask someone in your line of business who looks like they're doing well and see what they recommend.

Being choosy

I gained great experience in being choosy and setting expectations when I was juggling the business and my part time job. Now it's a case of juggling projects large and small – my Gantt chart (see Appendix 2) is my friend here, but so is being honest about myself and my abilities. I worked out that around 40 billable hours is the maximum I can really do in a week – it's hard work that involves a lot of concentration, and that's not counting admin time. I am lucky enough to have a few people I can recommend a prospect to if I can't take on their work, and I am getting better at doing that rather than taking too much on. That way, I can make sure I do a good job for my customers, and keep reliable for my regulars.

Diary Entry 28 February: Keep calm and carry on???

In which it gets a bit much.

I should be heaving on with another big chunk of work right now, but I need to decompress a bit and take stock. This is a bit of a rambly diary entry which I have used to work things out in my head a bit.

So, Libro's doing really well – too well, in a way. Yes, you can be doing too well. Not in that "I feel too well: oh, heck, I'm going to have a migraine" way, but in that "I actually have a little too much work to do right now" way.

And I am organised. I have my famous Gantt chart, in which I book either regular work (like the magazine that I know will come to me around the 14th of each month), my regular g clients who let me know their deadlines in advance, or work booked way in advance (usually student dissertations and theses). I also block in work I wasn't expecting as it comes in to me, and I colour it in, so that when it's in, it's in red, I know I need to do it, but I also have a visual reference of the work that's in and when it's due. This is really helpful for knowing which order to do my work in and I can see my deadlines, the weekends, etc., at a glance. I would go badly wrong without this!

Several categories of work come in to me:

Regulars who can send me big chunks of work, BUT I always have the option to say no. I can literally tell them what I can take and what I can't. One of these is my big transcription client. I know when the next conference is, and I know that when that comes up I can look at what work I have booked in and say "I can take x hours of transcription to do by 9.00 tomorrow morning". Similarly, I work for a student proofreading company. They get in touch to say they have x number of words to do, or they tell me when busy times are coming and I email in the morning and say "I can take 10,000 words today" and that's fine. With both of these clients, I feel I can say no: they have a pool of other people who can work for them, too, so no guilt, no worry.

Non-regulars who have booked in advance. If they know when their deadline is, they don't usually need a mad and terrifying turnaround time, so I book them in with a nice big space so I know I have room to move them around if I have something urgent in (this is why I charge extra for urgent work for these people: if it's urgent, it's on a shorter time scale and I can't move them).

Non-regulars who haven't booked in advance. If they are a potentially useful or interesting client who I can fit in now and would like to add to my roster, I agree and do the work. If I really cannot fit them in, or they don't fit my skillset exactly, I have a group of trusted people I can refer them on to. If it's a student dissertation, I'll drop Linda a line. If it's video transcription, off it goes to Michelle.

Regulars whose work is always urgent. This is my tricky category (1). Let me state here and now that I like working with them. They have interesting work, they appreciate my hard work, and they pay on time: maybe all three! There are a few translators/translation agencies whose work is usually urgent, however it's also usually short and doesn't take too long. Then I have a couple of clients who send me larger projects. Quite often, this involves me dashing back home from a cafe or zipping upstairs from the sofa – or there's an email to M to say I won't be around this evening … again. These clients don't have another proofreader / editor type person. I am the only one set up to help them.

Previous clients with a little more work … that isn't often little and is often urgent. This is my tricky category (2). I worked for them before, I know how their document works … so I should do it. But they are on my old pricing schedule and I feel I should honour that …

So, here's my problem. I enjoy my work (on the whole). I am happy to work hard for my clients. I am happy to put in THE ODD 11-hour day for them. But I do not want to work all the hours there are and tire myself out. I don't want to put back my gym trip or eat cereal at 2.30 pm for lunch. I do not want a chaotic day. I want to do the things I did this for: freedom to read, review, exercise, have my life back after working two jobs for a few years.

What do I do? I am not prepared to employ people on an employed or contractual basis. There is not enough work all the time to do this, and the administrative burden is large. I'm going to write a "Where next?" post soon, but just assume I will not be taking anyone on permanently. Managing expectations is all very well, but these clients need the work quickly, and I can't make infinite deadlines for my less urgent clients: their work has to be done at some time!

I think I need to instigate a back-up plan. After all, I might get really poorly, or want to – shhh – go on HOLIDAY one day. I am not indispensable and I know that is a problem I have dragged with me from my employed life: I am good at what I do, and reliable, so an assumption builds that I have infinite capacity and can take on this, and this, and this … I am good at saying no to new clients, now, but I need to know how to work with current ones.

How to relieve the pressure

It had all got a bit much for me at this stage. Lots of work, lots of different clients, and I will admit that I was doing better than I thought it would, and it all got a tiny bit scary.

First I needed to source another couple of people I could refer on to. I needed someone with good corporate experience, a marketing person who was also good at editing, a transcriber. I would prefer this to be someone I know. Also I wanted to be able to avoid them poaching my good clients, although obviously if the client wanted to move, that's up to them.

So I needed people to pass on new, one-off enquiries on to, who I could trust to do a good job. Then I needed to arrange with my clients that we had a back-up person to cover me. I would hopefully get first choice over the work and take it if I could: if I couldn't, I would refer it on to a named, reliable, hand-picked partner. But then their relationship with my client was their own, they invoiced them, and that's that, nothing more to do with me, for that job. This would be similar to not taking on a job but recommending a friend, and in fact the transcription company now uses two other transcribers I have recommended, so I knew that that worked OK in principle.

Bottom line: I didn't want to let anyone down, but I also didn't want to let MYSELF down.

Read on to March to find out how I sorted myself out!

March

In March, I got some resolution on the problems that were worrying me in late February, I also picked up a new client, based in Slovenia, who wanted me to work on smoothing out translations into English and started sending me some interesting projects. I was becoming increasingly passionate about helping people to realise that self-employment doesn't have to mean scary entrepreneurship, and started writing a series of articles on this topic aimed at other small business owners.

Keeping calm and carrying on

You've read my diary entry from February when I had a mini panic about how much work I had …

Many of my blog readers were kind enough to read and comment on this post where I wondered out loud how to manage a slightly-too-busy schedule. I had loads of advice and was also mulling over various options I had put together. Things started to go a lot better and more calmly, even though I had my busiest week to date in March!

Managing regular urgent work

I had a breakthrough when I managed to organise back-up for a couple of those clients who are regulars, and great customers, but sent me often large files at often short notice. I had already raised the "what if I'm busy, what if I want to go on holiday" issue with them, but we hadn't got round to discussing it further. Not their fault, not my fault, just timing. Then – crunch time – I have a big semi-regular project on. And a big file came through from a regular. In consultation with the client, I sourced someone who could do the work, explained the task to my colleague and provided a little support for this colleague as they did it (it wasn't quite the sort of work they are used to). I was pleased to find that a) the client was happy with the work; b) my colleague was happy doing the work; c) it worked fine to have them invoice the client direct; d) the client was a good payer so everyone was happy there; and e) the client was happy for this person to provide emergency cover in the future. Hooray! This just shows that persistence works, and that often solutions come through when there's a practical issue rather than just a theoretical one.

As my business has matured, I've passed some clients totally on to colleagues, as the way I worked changed and the nature of the working patterns in a typical week changed. This is where building up a network of trusted colleagues comes in really handy.

"Make them pay more"

A strong theme in the comments on the post was around making clients pay more in order to a) put them off and b) make sure I am being compensated adequately. I had adjusted my prices in January of this year as I had been under-charging. I moved editing and proof-reading work onto a full per-word rate, allowing for more predictability, and started charging a more fair rate (for me!) for the writing services I offer. I told my clients in advance what was happening with my charging, and all were fine and happy.

Turning down work

I was doing this already and continued – anything that looked like it would be a one-off small job (and I didn't have time to do it right then) or was not part of my core set of services, from now on got referred on to a colleague. In the first few weeks of this new policy I turned down a couple of small localisation jobs, passed on some student enquiries to a recommended friend, and passed on the opportunity to do some virtual assistant work for a current client, directing her on to another recommended friend who is now doing well providing that service to her.

Getting support

I was quite amazed how much just writing that Keep Calm and Carry On post helped me sort things out in my head. I was good at letting current regulars know when I have a big project on (that's just good customer service, I think) and better about talking through individual issues with business colleagues already, but I was also inspired to set up a local "networking" group (I was originally going to call it 'Café Of Pain', which I liked but some others didn't – it's now the KH Homeworkers' group) with a Facebook group and Twitter account which local people could use if they just need a quick coffee and a chat. This has grew to around a dozen members and I started to meet up regularly for "grown-up homework club" with one friend (we still do this: she does her language class homework and I work on my research project). It started making a difference just to know there were local people around one could call on or meet up with in an informal way.

In summary

    It's good to talk

    Solutions in business usually seem to come out of practical rather than theoretical situations

    Things started to get better and easier after a pinch point

    People who read my blog were (and are) marvellous

A typical week of full-time self-employment

Back in December, when I was still working at the Library 21 hours per week, I wrote about a typical week, so that I remembered what it was like trying to manage the two. Now I had settled into some kind of routine working at Libro full time, I repeated the exercise. So here's a "typical" week (if there is such a thing) of full-time self-employment (the Early Days version) …

Monday 19 March – got up just after 6, came up to the study, worked on a blog post then got down to finishing off proofreading the third chapter of a PhD a client was sending me in batches. I also put the finishing touches on a localisation I'd done for a big newish client – the client had answered some questions and I updated my "translation" on the software accordingly, signed the job off and added it to their monthly invoice. I had breakfast with M before he walked to work. I then did some admin to do with an event I was speaking at, and settled down to a good session on another client's PhD. It was my exercise rest day, so I could get some good long working sessions in. I had a good, healthy lunch and went for a walk up the High Street to pick up a few things: a real benefit of working from home is being able to pop out the shops at quieter times in the retail day (I was also spending less, although I'm not sure how, as I've never been a big spender anyway) and lunch and day time trips out are a good, healthy habit since I sorted out my Homeworkers' Resolutions (see Appendix 3). Back home and I had a few little bits in from regulars before doing another localisation session followed by some more PhD. I popped out to meet M on his walk home then had a quiet evening, interspersed with the odd email from a client, dealt with on my Blackberry.

Tuesday 20 March – I had some work in overnight – three student essays, two from people I was taking through their Master's course.

Oh, the luxury: if this had been in the Old Days, I'd have been frantically working on my previous projects before starting these. I completed one and started another before breakfast: while putting the bibliography of the first one in alphabetical order, I was inspired to put together a blog post on how to do that, so I created the screen shots and a draft blog post for that before getting on with the next essay. After breakfast I responded to a few emails asking for price and service quotations before continuing with student essays. I went to the gym, booked in another job with a regular client which involved downloading and learning some new software, and after lunch met an editing friend for a walk in the park and a chat about business – she's someone I recommend academic enquirers on to when I'm too busy to take them on and we needed to discuss a few things, and it was nice to do that in the sunshine. Then back to my desk for another editing session for some regular clients. I then ended up struggling with some recalcitrant software which meant I got behind and had to spend some of the evening after dinner working.

Wednesday 21 March – up early as usual and a couple of hours of PhD editing before breakfast. I realised the table numbering in the thesis had gone awry so emailed the client with the options. After breakfast I published my blog post on adding Contents Pages to Word, publicised that and continued with the thesis. I popped down to the Post Office depot to pick up a parcel and then up to the cafe for a catch-up with a fellow freelancer and friend. It's good to sound off about how things are going and chat about plans as well as just relaxing and seeing a human face. Came home and did a quick edit of a text translated from Chinese, and after lunch wrote a press release for a medical client. I worked some more on the PhD, went to the gym and did a little more after dinner. I explained why I've got to pay my tax twice next year to M (oh, the thrills! I've commissioned an article on Paying On Account from a great accountant I met recently for the Libro blog). A good balance today although another evening spent away from "family time".

Thursday 22 March – I worked on an academic article in the morning, including checking all the references were there (they weren't) and tracking down the missing ones, as well as making sure everything conformed to the author guidelines set out by the journal the article was being written for. That was fun and a bit more challenging than some of my work. A few payments in (including a big one I've been waiting for anxiously, which achieved my targets for this month and next!) and I checked a press release for a regular before getting down to working in the Scrivener software for my author client – I'm helping her combine her articles into a book. She's provided lots of guidance for me on what she wants, which is marvellous and very helpful! I also put a wash on – how lovely to be able to see the sun and get the washing out: I'd have been in the office this time last year, looking at the sun and knowing it wasn't drying anything on my line! I then walked in to the University (3 miles), got my hair cut and walked back again (3 miles) before doing a couple of hours of PhD work in the evening. I was thrilled to have the guest blog post on Tax Payment on Account I had commissioned come in to me by the end of the day.

Friday 23 March – I'd received lots of requests to do projects in through the evening and, in fact, the night, so had to crack on: finished proof-reading an advert and localising some company communications before breakfast, then published a troublesome pair blog post, wrote an article about a man and his dentistry, localised some information on electric cars and finished the big thesis I'd been working on all week. Phew! Another wash out on the line, lunch and then a couple of hours on some more chapters I'd had in from my other thesis client, before treating myself to an hour on my Iris Murdoch project in the cafe then meeting a contact to chat about some writing she'd like me to do for her website. I went to the gym and was set to do some more work after dinner, but unfortunately a house-related mini-emergency took up the rest of the evening, leading me to cancel plans for Saturday afternoon. Nothing changes there, then …

Saturday 24 March – This is where it gets tough. A late evening and then disturbances related to neighbours in the night meant I had to drag myself upstairs to the study to try to complete the work I'd promised my client by mid-morning, which I should have got on with the night before. I had at least written up my Saturday freelancer chat, so that was ready to just publish and promote before breakfast time. Fortunately, the first work project was continuing with a PhD I was fairly familiar with, so I could press on, knowing I was already aware of the writer's style and common errors. If I'd been too tired to do it, I wouldn't have, but I was just weary, and worked on it as well as I would normally do (maybe a little more slowly: I'm glad I charge by the word and not by the hour nowadays as it would have been hard to work out what to charge!). I finished that, sent off the chapters, worked on an issue of a magazine and put in a couple of hours on my author's blog-to-book project: I did also go for a walk in the park and didn't work after dinner time.

Sunday 25 March – Oh no: the clocks changed! I also found out I had a community meeting in the afternoon, so I didn't get the lie-in I'd hoped for (but I couldn't sacrifice my run). I finished my author's work and started a new PhD chapter, did my run, had lunch, finished the PhD chapter and sent it off, then started a transcription project I have had in from my student proofreading company – 5 hours of lectures to type up for a student (!). I got on quite well, so not too much worrying about finishing it. I also had quite a long piece of work from one of my translator clients, which came in just as I sat down to watch the TV with Matthew …

Conclusions

It was still a juggling act – between work, personal and social life and exercise. But it's not between work, work, personal life and exercise, at least. Not having fixed, monolithic hours to go to the office was making things a lot easier, although it was easier to cancel fixed items like networking meetings, which I really shouldn't do. I still got tired, and I still worked a few evenings, but if I work in the evening it's often because I've done something in the day time: it's rare for me to truly put in a 10-hour day! In terms of working hours, I did 40 billable hours that week, with perhaps another 7 or 8 admin hours. So that is actually about 6-7 hours more than before, although without the commuting time. Note that I did 35, 18 and 36 hours in the other weeks this month: there was no such thing as a typical week.

It felt better than my week before: it was definitely paying better, per hour and generally, and I did have more flexibility.

On (not) taking risks

What do you think of when you think of an entrepreneur? Richard Branson grinning from a hot air balloon basket, secure with his millions? Those people who started off selling eggs when they were 3 and were always selling something, so now they've got an empire? I started thinking about what an unlikely entrepreneur I am. I never showed a flair for business as a child. I kept my head down, did mainly admin jobs; was a good problem solver and solid worker, but not that exciting or, frankly entrepreneurial. Did anyone who knows me see Libro coming, and being the success it is now?

I think there are different ways of being an entrepreneur. Some people throw everything into it and take lots of risks. Others, like me, are more careful. And maybe we won't get the multi-million rewards (and the failures, and the lack of time for family and friends, and the stress …) but we're still brave.

I started my business. I didn't know what was going to happen. But I didn't take a risk with my finances and lifestyle: I 'soft-launched', starting the business part-time. Some people think doing this shows a lack of commitment – I don't think I show a lack of commitment to Libro, but I do want to protect my own interests while proceeding with the business.

I went part-time at my day job. But I wasn't taking too much of a risk, because I made sure I was making enough money with Libro to cover the loss of earnings.

I reached out to potential clients via Twitter and Facebook. But I did it more personally, subtly, answering tweets for help, reminding people of what I'm doing, rather than taking out expensive ads on all the social media. I used social media and have gained clients through it, but at no cost apart from my time.

I certainly felt a bit nervous when I went to my first networking meeting. "Wear your normal business attire," they said. What? My pyjamas, or tracky bottoms and a hoody? But I suited up and went for it, and made some good contacts. Later on, I started going to the Social Media Cafe and then helped out at Social Media Surgeries. But I didn't risk a lot of money on expensive memberships, or put everything into one form of networking; at the time of my first meeting, I was working full-time still and could not have coped if I'd suddenly developed lots of new customers. And I still evaluated the cost-benefit analysis of the bigger networking groups, and actively sought new smaller, local ones to join.

So what I'm saying is, you don't have to go out all guns blazing. If you've got an idea for a business but you're not sure what to do next, think about it and start small. If you fail, you haven't risked everything and lost it. If you succeed, you can grow slowly and carefully. It won't work for everyone, but nothing does. This maybe offers an alternative to jumping in, if you're not a natural risk-taker.

April

April was a good month for picking up new clients. I took on one localisation job, only to part ways with the client later in the year because of issues with payments and invoices, but also started working with another translation agency and a company helping an online retailer to customise their search engine .

It was end of year and tax self-assessment time (for smug me) so I was quite preoccupied with those issues, as well as beefing up my offering to my readers by working on a resource guide and index to my two growing blogs.

I also had some photographs done by my friend, Adam, which gave me an opportunity to have a much better professional online image, something that can be very important.

End of year

In April, I came to the end of my financial year, which coincides with the UK financial year. I found that it was a time for reflecting and taking stock of things.

Peaks and troughs in work life

I had noticed by now that I was a lot more relaxed about the quieter times in my business life. I used to get nervy, thinking it had all somehow, miraculously, "gone away" and I was going to end up destitute in a gutter. Now I had a better understanding that work for individual clients does tend to go in peaks and troughs, and some of those troughs sometimes coincide. Most of my clients by now were regulars, so it would be rather odd if they all stopped sending me work at the same time, and I realised that if it did go quiet, I would be as busy as anything really soon.

So I started to be able to use this extra down time to chill out a bit: reading, walks in the park, normal household stuff. And the key to keeping a steady work flow is really to make sure that you diversify your clients a bit. This could be in terms of:

* Type of client – corporate, public sector, individual, academic. All have different calendars and different time scales

* Type of work – big jobs and little jobs. Think of it like stones and pebbles; a few big jobs, then fit in little ones around them. No big jobs: take on lots of little ones

* Location of clients – I work with people around the world. Financial years are different; different countries' own bank balances vary. Having clients around the world protects me from all but a completely global crisis

Tax time ... and Payment on Account time

This year was Double Tax Payment year (see Why I Do My Tax in April) so I was very glad that while I was working full time, I had saved up and stashed away enough money to live on for a year, in anticipation of running the business and eventually needing to support myself. It is possible to save, even on a smallish wage, but it did mean that I had to be careful. In 2009 and 2010 when I started the business and worked full time, I saved all my Libro money and some of my salary. In 2011 I managed to live on my part-time wages and not touch my Libro income; and this year I was living on the pot of money I'd pre-saved (made easier by being so tight with myself in the years before [come 2013 and I'm living quite nicely, with treats and holidays – there is an end to it!]. It's just about do-able, but having to make sure I took into account the Double Tax thing was bit annoying, and doubly so for M, who probably thought I'd be able to justify the odd holiday by now!

Why I do my tax in April

Many people I know who are self-employed or run small businesses submit their tax returns – and find out what they owe – AND pay what they owe – at the end of January each year.

I discovered early on that you don't have to do your tax return in a frenzy at the end of January, just before the deadline. You can do it as soon as you have all your stuff together. I used to have to wait for my P60 from the day job, but this year I had my P45 from December all ready and waiting. I keep my accounts up to date all year round and then just make sure I include everything I've invoiced up to the end of the year even if it hasn't been paid yet. I just have to get my Statements of Interest from the banks (this makes me laugh: my two banks combined a year or so ago. They use the same computer systems; even their online systems are almost identical. But Bank A will print out your Statements of Interest there and then, whereas Bank B insist on posting them to you. One for each account) and then I'm ready to go (you have to state all interest earned from bank accounts on your tax return, even though they are already taxed. The HMRC takes this into account when it tots it all up).

I don't do my Self-Assessment in April, just after the end of the financial year that it's for, to be smug and feel clever. This is why I do it:

So I can put aside my tax and know I've got it there when I need to pay it. As I said, the main reason is that I want to know what I owe and make sure I put it aside. I'm not going to PAY it until it's due (in January and July 2013), but it's put safely aside, as of this morning, in an account that pays interest.

To release funds to live on. I could also do with some more money to live on for the year. Now I know what the tax bill is, I can happily withdraw the rest of the money in my Libro account to my personal account (NOTE: this is because I'm a Sole Trader: it's a bit different if you're a Limited Company, and remember I'm in the UK), and I now know what I've got to live on until next April. Sure, I could take money out as I go along, and lots of people do that, but personally I like to know exactly what I can take – especially in this slightly confusing double tax year.

Because I could. I'm lucky in that I have a simple business model and I do my accounts as I go along, and I'm not VAT registered. So I could finalise my end of year accounts quite easily, and just had to wait for my statements of interest from my banks to come through. Other years, I've had to wait for my P60 to come from the library, but this time I had a nice P45 from December and copied the numbers from that. Next year, I won't even have to worry about that!

Paying on Account

This coming year I will start Paying On Account, which is a bit of a pain. I don't mind paying my taxes, but this does seem a bit mean, as I will basically have to give the tax man a percentage of my income (income tax and national insurance) on all of my Libro income (I earned exactly the threshold in my day job), twice (because of the Payment on Account thing). Basically, HMRC in the UK like to get you paying your tax bill in advance. To get you to this state, one year, once you're over a certain threshold, you have to pay your tax twice in one year. This is how it will work for me:

* April 2012 – do my tax return for 2011-2012 and put aside what I will be due to pay

* January 2013 – pay my tax for 2011/12 in full and pay another half again for 2012/13 (you see, I don't PAY it early, I just work it out early and put it aside!)

* April 2013 – do my tax return for 2012/13

* July 2013 – pay the other half of my tax for 2012/13 that was calculated from my 2011/12 tax

* January 2014 – pay my tax in advance for 2013/14 plus any difference between the 2011/12 tax burden and the 2012/13 tax burden (this could go either way)

So, every year you pay next year's tax and even up last year's tax in January, rather than just paying last year's tax. Once you've done the double one, it's just a single lump of tax per year.

My suggestions for you:

If you run your own business (and surely you won't have read this far if you don't??!!), I strongly suggest you ...

* Register to complete your self-assessment online[6] if you haven't done so already
* Finalise your accounts for the tax year that ends in April, in April
* Order your Statements of Interest from your banks (some will print these off, some need to send one for each account through the post) and get together any other documentation you need
* When you've received your letter confirming your online registration, complete your self assessment online
* Set aside the amount of tax you now know you will need to pay
* Relax, knowing what you've earned and what you owe
* Avoid the frenzy next January because YOU'VE ALREADY DONE IT!

Note: I am not your tax advisor. I am not an accountant. This information is for personal illustrative purposes only. Please consult an accountant or tax advisor or the HMRC if you have any questions, worries, queries or complications. I am not responsible for anything you do with your tax return or tax affairs.

---

[6] http://www.hmrc.gov.uk/sa/file-online.htm

Diary Entry 12 April: Working out my tax (incorrectly)

I am pleased to say that I had a nice surprise when I submitted my tax return. I went a bit wrong and wildly overestimated when I worked out what I thought I was going to owe. But even if it had been a nasty surprise, I'd still rather know what was going on and what I owed!

What did I do wrong when working out my tax?

I really thought that, given the Payment on Account thing, I was going to give back around 65% of my income from Libro. This was based on the following fallacies:

I thought I'd earned my personal allowance at my library job and that was that – actually I overpaid my tax on that job as I went along, and I thought it would be refunded to me personally, whereas it just (sensibly) came off the total tax amount I owed

You know when you are employed and the general rule is that if you knock 25% off your gross pay you'll pretty well come up with what you'll end up with after tax? Well I was working on that assumption, forgetting that includes National Insurance payments that I don't pay now (don't worry: I do pay others!)

I thought that NIC 4 National Insurance payments, which I have to pay now I'm earning a certain amount, a) were 12% and b) applied to my full profit. Actually they are a) 9% and b) apply to all profit over a certain threshold

Basically, I have ended up needing to give the tax man about 49% of my Libro income, rather than 65%. Which is quite a difference.

How the Payment on Account has worked out

I was really pleased and relieved to have a screen come up at the end of submitting the figures, which states very clearly:

* my tax burden for 2011-12 and how much I have to pay by 31 Jan 2013
* the half of my Payment On Account amount for 2012-13 that is also due by 31 Jan 2013
* the half of my Payment On Account amount for 2012-13 that is due by 31 Jul 2013
* It's all very clearly set out, which was something I was wondering about.

So that's it: done. Minimal fuss.

Not only did I earn what I would consider to be a Living Wage with Libro last year (quadrupling my profit from 2010-2011), but I also didn't lose as much of it to the tax man as I thought I would.

So, I am able to support myself with my freelance work. I didn't, to be honest, think I'd get to this point for a while. I'm not saying I'm rolling in money, but I'm certainly OK for the odd coffee out, and a holiday, although I'd be on a tight rein financially this year (because of the double tax thing) if I hadn't got some money saved up from when I was in full time employment.

I don't want anyone to think that I'm being smug or showing off about this. I'm proud of what I've achieved, and I've worked very hard, but mainly I'm writing this down to prove that it is possible to do this, if you plan carefully, work hard and stick with it. I'm not a natural entrepreneur, and I've had pretty much a zero marketing budget; I'm lucky enough not to have too many business outgoings, but I am proving that it can be done.

First action for this financial year: take M out for a slap-up meal (on me, not expenses!) to thank him for his patience and forbearance!

May

May was a good, solid month: plenty of work including lots and lots of quite hardcore transcription work. M was away a couple of times, but I coped. And I gained another music journalist client through recommendation from my original one, and had fun for the rest of the year transcribing his interviews with the great and the good, the fun and the boring of the rock and pop world.

Having a less stressful job also made me think about stress, especially as a friend in a traditional career was having some health worries. Of course, then I began to wonder if I was consuming every detail of my and my friend's lives in order to spit them out as blog posts and articles …

Is the stress worth it?

I was chatting to a business associate the other day. He's enjoying his high powered, highly stressful and, let's be honest, high earning position, managing all sorts of change, rushing around here, there and everywhere … or he thinks he is.

Actually, he's plagued by all sorts of niggling illnesses, and these have become worse recently. Nothing that's putting him in hospital, but things that are affecting his quality of life, outside work more than inside, and can't be ignored.

So, is it worth the stress?

Downsizing your life, downsizing your stress levels

I can claim to be a bit of an expert on this, from personal experience. Having been doing a management-level, fairly demanding job in London, when we moved to the Midlands I was determined to have "a job". In fact, we both agreed we would indulge ourselves for a year, M going back to postgraduate study and me looking for a basic level library job.

I had a bit of trouble, as a qualified librarian, getting a basic entry level job, but I did in the end. Lots of people said I would get bored; my managers tried to encourage me to apply for promotions I didn't really want. I'd been up the corporate ladder, and I knew that it suited me at the time to have "a job" rather than "a career", something that would pay the bills but allow me the resources and energy to enjoy my new life in a new city.

So that's what I did, and I was perfectly content for a good few years. In fact, having that lower-stress, lower-responsibility job allowed me to start up Libro and develop my own business.

Different career paths for different life stages

Now, I could have quite easily chosen to progress through the corporate ranks again, gone for those management jobs, gone for the higher salary, which is always a consideration, isn't it? But I decided to go this alternative route, and set up the business.

But I did that in as stress-free and risk-free a way as I could. I'd decided it wasn't worth the fear of going full-time at the beginning, the stress of having to scrape around for money to live on, etc. Instead, I lived very frugally, scraped together money to live on in advance, and launched Libro full time in January 2012.

Now I have a satisfying job, where I'm responsible to myself and my clients, no bosses, no employees. I earn more than I've earned in any of my corporate jobs, and, I can honestly say that, even running my own business, where every sick day means income and jobs lost, where I do sometimes put in an 11 hour day, I can claim what I know makes me happy:

* responsibility for myself and my clients

* no employees
* no office politics
* flexibility to juggle my day to fit in friends and exercise

I am as stress-free as I can be. And I have no stress dermatitis, no IBS, I'm fit and healthy and enjoying life.

I'm not boasting about this: it's taken time to know myself and know what I want, and it's taken hard work to get here, which hasn't always been the most fun I've ever had. But I'm in my own space now, not trying to jam myself into an inappropriate role, and I'm very much happier as a result.

Know yourself and make the change

Think of a butterfly emerging from the confines of its chrysalis. Whether what's confining you is stress or something else, such as lack of the confidence to break free, surely it's worth trying to achieve your potential and seeing what you can do ... if you just break out of the chrysalis.

My advice to you, if you think you're stressed, or you *don't* think you're stressed but your body does ...

*** Think about what you REALLY want. Is the money worth it? Yes, we all need money to live on, yes, economic times are perilous, but if you can save anything ahead of changing your lifestyle, do it.

*** Think about what you enjoy, what you need, and work towards claiming it.

*** Talk to close friends or colleagues. How do they see your stress levels? What solutions can they offer?

*** Talk to a reputable life coach or careers counsellor. What ideas do they have?

*** Mind-map, brainstorm, go walking for a week, whatever it takes to give you space to think this through.

*** Seek mentors and role models. People have told me my blog posts have helped them on their path to self-employment (hooray!) – look around for people doing what you might fancy doing, and drill down into how they did it.

*** Think laterally. Do you really want to be an architect, or do you want to work for a housing association? Do you really want to be a social worker, or do you want to train as a counsellor? Could you work part time while you pursue your aims?

My "career path", from corporate ladder-climber to "just a library assistant" to successful small business owner shows that you can step down, sideways, whatever. I'm not a risk-taker, I'm not particularly well-off, and it hasn't always been easy. But it can be done.

Good luck!

Diary Entry 18 May: Home alone

I've been Home Alone for the past just-over-a-week. Not only that, but it's been the longest that M and I have been apart since we got together over 10 years ago!

I thought it would be harder because I work mainly at home now, mainly on my own. I was a bit worried about turning "feral": you know, not obeying my rules for Home Workers, eating odd things at odd times, sleeping through the alarm, waking up at 6pm and thinking it was 6am and getting my days inside out, all that.

Actually, it was OK.

I think that, because I'm used to being on my own in the house during the day, it was easier during the evenings. Because it's lighter later, I was just up here in my study a lot, and when it did get dark, it was nearly bedtime, whereas I've been up here in the dark before M's even due home in the winter.

I also made doubly sure that I had something planned to do every day. Thanks to my super friends, this worked really well, and I was out of the house, spending time with different people, or having them round. I slept OK, I ate fine, and although I did miss Matthew, we "talked" every day via email, googlechat or Skype, so we were never that far apart.

So if you've started working from home and you're worried about that inevitable "home alone" time when it comes … here's the report from the other side of it: it's not too bad!

Good things about working from home in the summer

Although I got a bit irritated in May when I was low on work on rainy days and busy, busy, busy on sunny days, I realised that actually, compared to people working in offices, with other people, or both, I was pretty lucky.

- It doesn't matter what I wear (within reason – I do have windows in my office) and I can change part way through the day if I want to

- No window / fan / blinds wars – it's just me and the cat, and the cat doesn't really have a say in which windows are open. Every office has window open/closed, fan on/off and curtains or blinds open/closed wars and it's liberating to be able to do whatever I choose

- If I really want to, I can start working at 5 am and have a siesta after lunch

- I can have lunch in the garden

So no more bemoaning for me. I'm lucky to be busy … and I'm lucky to be able to keep comfortable in the heat and to be able to do what I need to do in order to keep comfortable.

June

In June we had the Queen's Diamond Jubilee. After trying not to get TOO involved in the local street party, I somehow found myself making 150m of bunting – all by hand. But it was nice getting involved with the neighbours and all working together, and my unconventional hours made it easier for people to drop by with triangles of cotton or rolls of tape, as you do!

My unconventional hours did cause me to pause and think, though, about how different the life of the self-employed person is from that of the employee. So there was a lot of musing about what I do in the day, and in the month. Even if you don't work from home, I bet you don't take as much notice of public holidays as the worker bee …

On bank holidays

When you work in an office, Bank Holidays (or public holidays, or whatever you call them in your country) are really important. There's lots of discussion about what you might do on the Bank Holiday, and what you did, afterwards. Lots of chat about "don't forget not to come in on Monday". People who have odd working schedules get upset or pleased about how Bank Holidays are treated in their pay and holiday schedules (if you don't usually work on a Monday, do you still get an extra holiday, etc., etc.)

If you're a freelancer or run your own business, especially if you work from home, alone, let me tell you that Bank Holidays disappear into the ether. They do not matter. They might as well not exist, except that a) there might be extra people around the house, startling you with their presence occasionally, and b) people might expect you to be free to do stuff.

I'm not sure if this is limited to people who, like me, have a lot of international clients whose public holidays are at different times to ours. But I bet anyone with a big project to complete doesn't stop just because it's Bank Holiday Monday. I coped OK with the double one for the Jubilee, but the early May one was a different story. Up the stairs I popped at 6 am, as usual. "See you at 8 for breakfast," I cheerily called to M, as usual. "Eh? What?" I'd completely missed the memo that there was a Bank Holiday. Oh, because there are no memos when you work alone ...

By the way, I have been known to check what day it is, or whether it's morning or afternoon, when entering the gym, for example. I know which column I'm in on my Gantt chart, and I'm never startled by my deadlines, but I did find myself hoping that other home / lone workers are the same and I wasn't starting to go a bit odd ...

A typical day for Libro

It was great working for myself full time, but sometimes I was reminded that not everyone realises that, just because I might mention I was working at, say 6am, and again at 10pm, that didn't mean that I was working as such for the whole day. If I was, that would be a bit worrying, of course. Anyway, it was half way through the year and time to note down a "typical" day in my life now.

A typical day now

6.00 – 8.00 Get up. Check email and work for about 90 minutes.

8.00 – 9.00 Breakfast with M. Shower.

9.00 – 9.30 Check and answer emails, check Facebook and Twitter. Publish a blog post.

9.30 – 11.00 Work of various sorts – projects large or small

11.00 – 11.30 Cuppa and a drink of squash. Emails and admin

11.30 – 12.30 More billable hours

12.30 – 14.30 An hour at the gym, lunch and shower

14.30 – 16.00 Work.

16.00 – 16.30 A soft drink, a cuppa (a bun?) and some emailing.

16.30 – 18.00 Work.

18.00 – 19.00 Either work or walk down to meet M on his way home from work

19.00 – 20.00 House admin and dinner.

20.00 – 21.00 Maybe an hour of work if I'm busy or have tight deadlines. Otherwise, TV etc.

21.00 – 22.00 TV or reading.

22.00 – 22.30 Check email, last minute bits and bobs, check personal email

22.30 – 23.00 Get ready for bed, a bit of reading.

23.00 Bedtime.

So that gives me between 7 and 9 billable working hours – usually more like 7, which is what people do in an office, of course, just not so spread out through the day.

And in a week of days like this I will get out to the cafe to meet friends at least once, pop into town or meet a friend for dinner, and have some time writing up blog posts, etc.

Writing this list got me musing about "presenteeism" and the way it creeps into self-employment.

Having inadvertently given my friends and family the impression I work all day and every day, I started to think about whether the cult of "Presenteeism" is as strong in the self-employed community as it is among employees. Surely it shouldn't be ... and if it is, what can we do about it?

On presenteeism

What is presenteeism?

We've all heard of **absenteeism**, or the practice of regularly removing oneself from the working environment for no good reason. **Presenteeism** is the opposite. It's in the Concise Oxford English Dictionary, and here's how they define it:

"The practice of being present at work for longer than required, especially as a manifestation of insecurity about one's job",

This manifests itself in that classic competition over who can stay latest in the office (or, more importantly, who can be *seen* to be staying latest in the office. Or being in earliest. Or both. We've all sent an email to the boss when we've got in particularly early, haven't we?

Now, that's all well and good when you have a boss to impress. But what if you work on your own? And I'm admitting doing this myself, here – although inadvertently. It's easy to send that Tweet or Facebook status at the end of a long day ...

"Phew – done 10 hours at the desk today – big project!!!!"

but is it so easy to say

"Good day, did a couple of hours of work, all caught up so I lay around reading for a few hours"?

Well, is it?

Why do we have to engage in presenteeism?

I'd be interested to work out why we do this. Are we so busy trying to combat that insidious view of freelancers as people who sit around in their pyjamas watching daytime telly? Surely our friends and family know we don't do that by now?

If you work in an office, you will tend to have set start and finish times, a proper lunch break, and weekends off (or a set working pattern) and holidays. How many freelancers take the full holiday entitlement they would be given as an employee? I know I probably don't.

So when it's quiet, we're up to date and we skip off merrily to the cafe, or the gym, or just lounge in the garden for an hour or so, is that really a crime?

And isn't it better for our friends and family to know we're happy. whole, balanced and relaxed than working every hour there is on a hideous treadmill of work? Didn't at least some of us go freelance to avoid that hideous treadmill of work?

Celebrate balance, not overwork

I'm not suggesting we stop working when we need to be working. Everyone has to pull one of those 11 hour shifts sometimes. But let's all be honest about how we live, celebrate the downtime as well as the busy times, and acknowledge that, yes, we do do this in order to have balance and flexibility in our lives, and we do have work patterns which are different, but balanced over the grand scheme of things.

Update: I did get better about a) taking time off and b) talking about it – read on for more about how this worked out.

July

July was another busy month with a new localisation client coming on board and associated software to learn (localisation involves "translating" US English into UK English. It can be done in Word, using Track Changes, in two columns in Excel, or using the kind of complicated software that translators use. But it's all good for keeping the brain supple and flexible!

The beginning of July also marked six months being full-time self-employed, so I had a think about how it was all going. I knew I was hitting my targets – and more – but I wanted to stop and consider how I was feeling about it all, too.

Diary Entry 02 July: The first six months

Wow – the end of June on Saturday marked the end of my first six months running Libro full time, with no safety net of an office job (but plenty of safety nets in terms of savings and experience!).

I thought I should mark this in some way, so I changed the photo on my Facebook page[7] to give myself some flowers, and I'm writing this to review the past six months. Has it gone as expected? Has anything surprised me? Am I actually doing OK? Am I happier? Am I enjoying myself? What have I learned?

Has it gone as expected?

In a word: no!

But in a good way. Each time I dropped a day at the office job in 2011 I experienced a small "slump" where the work coming in, and the profit made, dipped a little, just for a month. So I expected a big

---

[7] http://www.facebook.com/libroediting

drop, a fallow period, especially as I had Jury Service to contend with at the beginning of January.

In fact, to tell you the truth, I was quite looking forward to a little rest. I'd actually finished my library job on 12 December and had worked solidly since then, gaining a new client and working over Christmas, including through a cold! But ... it didn't happen. I had obviously gathered a good number of regular customers, and adding a new one into the roster made a big difference. Also, some of my regulars increased the work they sent to me, as I had told them I was more available now, and having more hours available to work made me able to, well, do more.

Basically, the work ramped up right away, and I've been working pretty well full-time hours ever since!

Did anything surprise me?

I have to admit that I'm a little surprised that I'm sitting here, working full time on my business, keeping busy and earning well. I didn't think I was going to FAIL as such, because I had planned everything out, and by the end of March I knew that I was earning enough to keep myself going. But I'm actually doing better than I'd expected, in terms of busy-ness and in terms of income.

I think I've surprised myself with my success – a few years ago, I could never have dreamed I'd be doing this! I'm not being smug about it and it has come with a LOT of hard work, and I should have had the faith in myself not to be surprised at this point ...

Have I surprised anyone else, I wonder? Friends who've known me for years and newer business friends? Yes, I had, they said: but they knew I could do it and they were proud of me for doing so. I love my friends!

Am I actually doing OK?

In terms of income, I'm happy to admit that I'm earning more than I have in any other job I've had (only a little more than the highest-paying one, but still). And now I've got through the double tax year and out the other side with my tax payments safely set aside, knowing what I owe and what I could take home, I am taking home enough to live on and to treat myself (and my patient friends who graciously accepted cheap / badly planned / cheap AND badly planned Christmas and Birthday presents for a few years). I'm not rolling in it, and I have turned into neither Richard Branson nor Mrs Thatcher, but I'm doing well enough to be happy with it.

In terms of clients, I have a fairly full roster of regular clients of various kinds, keeping my work varied, from editing non-fiction and fiction books to transcribing international conferences and journalists' interviews to localising web and marketing text for all sorts of companies. My website and blog are getting more hits every month, and I do like looking at those stats!

Physical health wise, I'm eating well and getting to the gym a lot more, walking to meet Matthew after work, etc. Mental health wise I am a lot less stressed and I thrive on working on my own but having virtual colleagues via social media and business contacts and friends via various networking groups. I also have more flexibility and time to see friends and spend time with family.

Another important thing for me is helping people and giving back. I've been able to put together some great resources for students, Word users and other small businesses[8] – OK, they bring people to my website, but I also love being able to help people out. My Saturday freelance/small business chats[9] are going well, with a year's worth done so we're onto a combo of updates and new

---

[8] http://libroediting.com/blog/students-small-businesses-word-users/
[9] http://libroediting.com/2011/06/11/freelancer-chat/

interviews. I love being able to showcase other small businesses and share our stories with people thinking about making the leap into self-employment or business ownership. And I've been able to help out other businesses and groups at the Social Media Surgeries,[10] etc., too.

Am I happy / enjoying it?

Yes, I am! I'm so much happier and relaxed than I was even before I was working part time and running the business part time. This kind of lifestyle really suits me, and I genuinely enjoy the work. It's great to be able to use my abilities and stretch myself, and I love knowing I have those regular clients out there and hearing how they are getting on and interacting with people all around the world, from China to Canada.

Specifically related to the full-time aspect of it, I love the fact that I do have more time for other projects, reading, M and friends now. It might not look like it sometimes, but I am working fewer hours compared to when I was employed and self-employed at the same time. And I'll admit that it's nice to have a bit of money after a few years of hard saving and being very frugal indeed.

What have I learned?

The most important lessons I've learned are …

* Embrace new opportunities, whether that's new kinds of client, new kinds of work, presenting at training days or whatever
* Don't worry if it goes a bit quiet: it will pick up again and I can use the time to recharge my batteries
* I can do it – and I must trust in myself and my relationships with my clients that I can

---

[10] http://libroediting.com/2011/04/13/helping/

* Eat a lunch made of more than one food group before 2pm and go outside every day and all will stay reasonably well and healthy (see my Homeworker's Resolutions in Appendix 3)

Here's to the next six months ... and onwards!

On mutual support

I was invited to present at a training morning on small business and social media. I'm always happy to help other small businesses and community organisations learn about the things I've picked up over the years, and, while presenting my case study as a business person who has used social media to get an audience and clients, I emphasised the idea of mutual support.

I talked mainly about retweeting on Twitter and also about the way I feature other small businesses in my "Small Business / Freelance Chat"[11] posts on my blog. I also talked about how some editing colleagues (who I do NOT see as competitors) kindly shared some of my blog posts on various forums to which they belong, which helped a couple of my posts go "viral" (500 hits in a couple of days is a big deal to me).

So I just wanted to take a moment to mention some of the kind instances of **support** I've had from other people in the editing / small business community (and, of course, encourage you to look at their resources too).

Editing colleagues regularly share my Facebook and Twitter posts and link to my articles on their websites, forums they frequent, etc. (and of course I do the same for them, too)

Journalists sometimes come to me for interviews, soundbites and opinions. I always make sure they put a link in anything they publish

---

[11] http://libroediting.com/2011/06/11/freelancer-chat/

online, then I return the favour and share their article with my friends and contacts

Colleagues in editing and the small business world and I comment on each other's blog posts, agreeing, disagreeing, never spamming but always letting people know who we are and where we come from. We also write guest blog posts for each other on appropriate issues and topics

All of these different posts in different places give me …

A **new audience** who may not have come across me yet

The chance to **help more people**, as well as to **market myself** to them – both are truly equally important to me

Link-backs, i.e. my URL on their page – Google likes these as they confirm that the site being linked to is valid and useful – so it helps me in their search results

And all this is on top of the **retweeting and Facebook sharing** (see why that is important to small businesses in On Social Media and Networking).

If you have a Twitter account, a Facebook account, a website or blog, **do share other people's resources** – it's really worthwhile and can make a friendly small business person very happy!

Paper is sometimes best!

I was looking at the Society for Editors and Proofreaders website and musing about how I almost never do work on paper manuscripts (once in well over 500 jobs), and then the doorbell rang and my new to do list stationery had arrived … so that's one thing where I do stick with paper.

Well, one of two things.

With my to do lists, I have flirted with Google Calendar / Tasks and I do put meetings, events and appointments like Skype chats or phone calls in there. But all through my working life, I have had a paper to do list, and, you know what? That's what I like to have. I had been using one of my few Libro notepads to keep it, but around this time bought a special book – appointments on the left hand page and Things To Do Today on the right. With tick boxes and everything. There is also room for notes, which is handy for those phone calls.

The other thing I keep on paper is my customer records. Not entirely: I keep a note of people's pricing and other terms as part of their contact details in my email account. As I do work for people, I either create an invoice for that piece of work, including details of the time spent or word count, depending on how I invoice them, or add the project to their current monthly invoice But I have an A4 spiral bound book with a section for each major client and one for one-off/student clients. This is where I note down the date, time, word count and charge for each job I do.

I like writing. I like pen and paper. I like using fountain pens with different colour inks. I might do all my editing, proofreading, writing and transcription on the computer, and I might have an online book review blog; I might even have a Kindle … but when it comes down to it, I read real books too (mostly, actually), write my book reviews in a nice notebook first, and keep paper records and to do lists.

You don't have to do what is most up to date and modern. Everything doesn't have to be In The Cloud. Do what you feel comfortable with!

August

August saw Libro's third birthday, and I chose an unconventional but deeply satisfying way to celebrate. I also acquired two more journalist clients through the power of recommendations via Twitter.

Another exciting development came when I published my first e-book[12] – I had wanted to have a go at this as I have a number of writer clients who were planning to publish electronically, and I wanted to see what their experience would be, and just how easy it was to do (it's really easy). I also had something to say about my efforts to lower my cholesterol, so that was the subject I chose, and I'm pleased to say that it's sold solidly, if not spectacularly, since, and helped a lot of people (which was the main point of the exercise).

I became aware that not everyone with a blog or website knew how to look at their viewing statistics, or how to interpret those, so put together a guide that I'm sharing with you now. But first, Happy Birthday, Libro …

Diary Entry 01 Aug: Happy Birthday, Libro!

I'm proud to celebrate Libro's third birthday today! In August 2009, I really had no idea that I would be working for myself full time, doing such varied things as transcription, writing and editing as well as thesis proofreading, which is what I started out doing.

I am going to have a small celebration at some stage soon, perhaps with friends of Libro, perhaps just with M. I was considering

---

[12] *How I Conquered High Cholesterol* – more information available at http://librofulltime.wordpress.com/reducing-cholesterol-naturally/

marking the occasion by buying myself something, perhaps a piece of jewellery. But then I had a better idea.

I've been doing Kiva[13] loans for a while now: we've got two loans on the go and re-loan them as they get paid back. Now I've helped to fund five more women entrepreneurs (which means those loans will be on-going too , helping more people as they get paid back). Kiva funds grassroots organisations that help people do small, sustainable things that will make a difference to their lives.

So, I've helped women in Paraguay to run their textiles business, a lady in Lebanon to sell food in Ramadan, some ladies in Mali to run various enterprises, a lady in Samoa to build up her spear-fishing endeavours and a lady in Georgia to run her business.

I've also made a donation to LUCIA,[14] a charity close to my heart, run by friends from the Library where I used to work, who do the same kind of work in Ethiopia. Much better than having something for myself!

Looking at your statistics

Do you ever look at your blog **or** website statistics? If you don't, I'm going to show you why you should. If you do, do you get all you can out of them? Do you look at them actively or passively?

Note: this post uses examples from the WordPress.com statistics pages, because that's the blogging/website platform I use. But all of the standard blogging sites, plus Google Analytics, Statcounter and other analysis tools will offer you similar information, with similar headings. For the full article on which this is based, plus illustrations, please visit the Libro blog.[15]

---

[13] https://www.kiva.org/
[14] http://www.luciacharity.org.uk/
[15] http://libroediting.com/2012/08/17/keep-an-eye-on-your-stats/

Why should I look at my statistics?

Looking at your statistics can help you **tailor your blog** to match what your readers want, and will also alert you to who is talking about you and where they are doing so. You can also measure the success of your attempts to build your audience through posting on social media and other blogs and sites. Here are some of the things you can find out …

* Which posts or pages are people looking at a lot … and which ones are they ignoring?
* Is there a kind of post that people are particularly interested in?
* When do people read your posts?
* How do people find you (social media, web searches …)
* What search terms do they use?
* Where do your readers go next – what links do they click?
* Are people finding your site via other sites and blogs?

How do I find and view my blog / website statistics?

Usually you'll have some kind of button or menu option called **Statistics** or Analytics. On WordPress, you will find a Stats option when you go into your blog, or you can click on the bar chart at the top of the screen. Once you've found them, you'll find a screen that gives you some basic details.

Now we've located our stats, let's look in more detail about what they can tell us.

How do I tell how many times my blog posts have been viewed?

One of the important ones to look at is your **most popular pages**. I can see at a glance what posts and pages have been popular (and if I click on **yesterday** or **summaries** I can see previous days' stats, while if I click on the magnifying glass next to the number, I can see all the views for that post). This is useful, as I can tell how I'm doing in the search engines, if it's an older post, or whether my alerts are doing well, if it's today's post going up the ratings.

How do I tell how people have found my blog or website?

It's very useful to know **how people are finding your blog**. You should have a section of statistics called something like **referrers** or **referrals**.

You can glean all sorts of information from this. I get most of my hits from **search engines**, then **Facebook** and **Twitter**, then a variety of websites and blogs that I'll go through in a minute. This has changed – when you're new to blogging, you'll get most of your hits from Facebook and Twitter and other social media, as your friends will be looking at your posts and you will be promoting them on social media. As your blog gets indexed on the search engines, results will start showing up from them.

Looking at the pages from which your readers have come can be SO useful. Here's what you can glean from them:

* Who is talking about you, and what are they saying? Got a random link from someone's website? Go and have a look – and make sure you thank them for talking about you!
* Who is talking about mentions you've given them on your website? Say one of the people I've featured on my blog puts something on her own blog about my feature, this gives me a great link-back that Google will like indexing.
* If you're using blog comments or answers on expert sites to get blog traffic, is this working? Are you getting hits through from those sites?

All good stuff, and I can say thank you to people who have sent readers my way, or even find out when they've done so (all these links can be clicked, so I can see exactly what people have said). Now, what about those search engines?

How can I find out what search terms people have used to find my site?

You should have a heading like **Search Terms** somewhere on your stats page. This offers a world of exciting information.

For a start, you can see exactly what people are searching for. It might be useful to change the wording on your blog posts to get further up the search results for a popular term. It's also worth searching for these terms yourself and seeing where on the Google results page they appear. Another useful point is it can give you ideas for future blog posts. I noticed that someone had found me while searching for Autocorrect, which I had mentioned in a blog post. So then I wrote a post on Autocorrect itself, which has been quite popular.

It can also be quite amusing to see what people search for. Someone once came through to my blog having searched for "persuasive piece on children believing in the tooth fairy" – I think they may have been disappointed (they found me because I mention the tooth fairy in an example sentence explaining a word definition).

How can I see where my blog readers are?

On WordPress you can see a rather nifty **world map** with the countries from which your visitors have come from highlighted.

This is more of a fun distraction than a useful tool, to be honest, but if you discover an anomaly, for example if you're in the UK and you get a lot of visitors from Brazil, you could consider tailoring some of your blog posts for this market. I get a lot of international visitors, so I'm going to make sure I talk about my work with non-native speakers of English soon.

Is my website traffic increasing? What did I do to make that happen?

As well as today's data, you can usually see **a month or year's worth**, too. If I look at the traffic on my website and blog over time, I can see that it started increasing at the beginning of 2011.

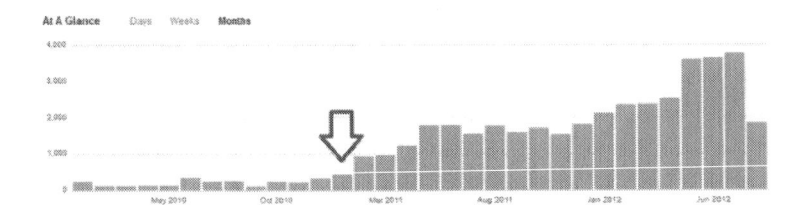

What did I do at the time of that **big arrow**? Started writing my blog!

Do people read my blog more at the weekends?

Looking at your **daily traffic** will show peaks and troughs. If your blog is more popular at the weekends, it might be good to post new content then. If I drill down into one of my blog posts, the ever-popular "What do I do if my comment boxes go tiny in Word?", I can see that it's not read very often at the weekends.

This says to me that office workers are looking for and using this post, so I can make sure I post more for that kind of audience and save other new posts for the weekends.

Where do my website visitors go when they leave my site?

This is usually found under the heading **Referrals**, or maybe **Click-throughs**. These fall into a few groups, in my experience …

Other resources belonging to you – I can see my visitors going through to my e-book(s) and my other blogs.

Websites you've mentioned in your blog. If you want to get the owners of those websites to give you a freeby or a mention, collect stats on how often you send readers their way, and ask away!

Links people have posted in your comments. Are too many of your readers moving on to a rival who's been commenting a lot? It's worth then talking to them about some mutual linking to make the traffic more fair.

So there we go. **Look at those statistics**, whether you're using WordPress or another host for your blog. And look at them actively: think about what they mean and how they can help you to find out how to **tailor your blog** to your audience and **drive more traffic** to your blog or website.

Diary Entry 31 Aug: A holiday from WiFi!

I agreed to go on holiday back in June – and M could only really take time off from his University department in August, so August, busy time for Libro, it was. I had enough notice to tell the clients who send me a lot of work in August, and it was only one week. Also, the hotel had WiFi so I'd be able to take a laptop and check in on my emails every now and again … right?

The night before our train trip up to Scotland saw me up to 1am finishing a localisation project for a client. I had until the Monday to do it, but Friday night saw me labouring away – and I'm glad I did.

The hotel did not have reliable WiFi. Worse still, it turns out that the Highlands of Scotland aren't best for mobile coverage, so even my trusty BlackBerry was worse than useless. Hunching over a smartphone while bumping down a glen in search of eagles is not really good use of one's time (or particularly polite) so I was basically out of contact with regulars and new clients for a week. A week!

How did I cope?

* I swallowed it. There wasn't really anything I could actually do about it, so I accepted it.
* I had Out of Office on and I managed to tweak it to advise that I wouldn't see any messages until my return.
* I managed to sneak through a message to each of my regulars to tell them I wouldn't be able to do anything for them.

And then I relaxed and enjoyed my holiday, ate, slept and read, and had a very nice time and a well-earned rest, and came back renewed and energetic!

September

September is traditionally a busy month as it's the month when Master's students hand in their dissertations. I had a few of those and some from a student proofreading company I work for, but I also gained two new clients, both translation agencies for whom I check the English of their translations for adherence to the norms of British or American English. I spent quite a lot of September working on texts aimed at training people in the tourist industry in Eastern Europe to communicate with British guests, which was fun!

I was also busy with extra-curricular activities, too, presenting a paper at a conference, and getting a good insight into how my academic clients feel when they are doing that. It's always useful to put yourself in your clients' shoes every now and then …

On social media and networking

It's time to talk about social media and live networking and why they're similar in so many ways. If you run a business, here are some hints about how they work and how you can also help fellow businesses to use them. If you have friends who run businesses, see how you can help them extend their reach and help more people.

Whether I'm talking to an individual at a networking event, tweeting a link to a blog post or updating my status on Libro's Facebook page, I'm (hopefully) addressing two audiences. The first is the person I'm speaking to. And the second is the people to whom they could potentially carry my message.

Networking events, co-working sessions, Twitter followers, Facebook friends – what they have in common is that each is a network. Think of it like pyramid selling or chain letters but in a good way. X knows 2 people who know 2 people each, that's 4, each of those know two people and that makes 8 – even if some of them know each other, the network doubles each time. Or rabbits. It's a bit like rabbits, too ...

These networks are more diverse and varied than you might at first think. Even if you're close to someone in your life, history or profession, it is unlikely that your network overlaps with theirs completely. Some examples ...

* My partner of 10 years – I have 224 friends on Facebook, he has 93, but we only share 41 of those people.
* A Birmingham friend interested in the same things as me has 161 friends – and only 80 of them are shared with me.
* An old University friend who is a freelancer like me has just 8 mutual friends out of a total of 239.
* Similarly, Libro has a certain number of individual "likers" plus businesses, so I make sure I share some of my Libro updates with my wider circle of friends.
* It's the same on Twitter – I'm pretty sure that not all my friends' followers are following me (although it's harder to extract the figures there), so if I retweet a business's message, my followers will see their message, and if they retweet mine, theirs will know about me.

When I'm at a networking meeting, I'm aware that the person I'm talking to is not always likely to want to buy my services. But it's very likely that, if I've made a good impression on them, they will remember me, and when they come across someone else in their social or business network who needs something that I offer, they will recall my details and pass my information on. There's lots of research on how to ensure that happens, but the general principle stands.

In the same way, if I tweet or put up a Facebook update about something Libro's doing, the people who see it directly from me probably know all about what I do, or they might not need a proofreader or transcriber right now. But if they "share" the Facebook post or retweet the tweet, who's to know who out of their wider circle might find it useful?

Much of my work comes through personal recommendation, usually from previous clients, but also through networks of friends and associates. This isn't a plea to share and retweet my stuff, though ... it's a general reflection on how you can help your friends with businesses small and not-so-small to grow their networks and get known about. Even large organisations need this – I was talking to someone from a museum just the other day, and he was bemoaning the lack of likes and shares on their Facebook page. Which is, by the way, good, engaging and interesting.

Hopefully this post has made some entrepreneurs, and most importantly their friends, aware of just how important the power of networks can be to their businesses. Share a post or a tweet by a friend, a charity you support, a business you like ... and someone in your network of contacts might find just what they need!

–

Postscript: Given the riots in the UK that happened in August, and the discussion on social media surrounding them, I thought I should say a few words on that subject. Social media – Twitter, Facebook and the like – are just another communication medium, like newspapers, letters and the telephone. Even if some newspapers print vile things, it doesn't mean newspapers in themselves are dangerous and evil. Poison pen letters don't lead to calls for paper and pens to be banned. Personally, during the riots, I saw many good things come through Twitter, in particular. My local pub and other people in my area tweeted out reassurances that all was quiet. The police and the Resilience Team sent out messages of calm and information, and we retweeted those to help damp down unsubstantiated rumours. I heard about the cleanup campaign through Twitter and would never have known about it without that medium. So don't worry that you're helping perpetuate some kind of evil empire if you retweet a message about a decorators or editor – it's just a communication channel!

Diary Entry 17 Sep: Back to school

The autumn is a traditional time of renewal and change for me. Decisions are made, changes are implemented. In the past I've bought a flat (and sold it), made plans to move in with my partner, left jobs and started jobs in the autumn. Of course I also made the big decision as to when to go full time with Libro last autumn! It always feels like the start of something; not the slow decline into winter, the ageing of the year, but a time of renewal, warmth indoors and frosts outdoors, time in my head, not time with the sun soaking into my skin ...

I think this is probably more to do with the UK academic year than anything else. And, in connection with that, this Autumn feels more than a little odd.

I did some pondering about this and I realised that there have been very few years in the 40 I've been on this earth so far in which I haven't had some kind of "back to school" feeling. And yet I don't have that this year. To break this down ...

1972-1975 – Too young for school!

1975-1992 – At primary then secondary school, then University, then working at the University Library.

1993-1995 – No back to school! Working in various jobs

1996-2004 – Working at EBSCO. Our renewals period was Sept-Oct each year, so that felt like the start of a new year all over again

2005-2011 – Working at the University Library. No, contrary to popular opinion, we didn't have the summer off, but of course back came the students after the pause of the summer vac, and it all started again ...

So that's, what, 7 years out of 40 when I haven't been somehow going Back To School in one form or another. No wonder I feel a bit odd!

Back to work

In some ways, this autumn does feel like going "back to" something. We had quite an odd summer, all in all. We had workmen in through the summer, not just lovely Terry the decorator, but a door man and a hedge man. This meant a change to my routine – as I am by default "The one who's at home" I had to be dressed reasonably normally, able to answer questions, and making decisions on all sorts of things. I had some time off work for the Olympics, but because we had a "real" holiday booked, I couldn't be as unavailable as I'd have maybe liked to be, so I ended up scrabbling around working between TV viewing, and it wasn't as satisfactory as it might have been.

Then we DID have our holiday, and that was lovely, and I learned that I CAN have an actual week away from the internet connection (and even phone connection) and Libro wouldn't dissolve into nothing.

And then I attended an academic conference and now I'm back and starting into the run of working life up to Christmas.

So, what's changed?

This is still my time of change and renewal, and I guess it always will be. Fine – some people's season of renewal is the spring, some the summer and mines' the autumn. What's yours? In a way, this feels like the start of Libro full time, more than January did. I've been able to reflect on the past 9 months, see what's worked and what hasn't, and have a think about the way forward.

There are no big changes coming, nothing exciting, nothing shocking. I do know I've been working a bit too hard, a few too many hours. Some of that is unavoidable – other people's deadlines slipping, and crashing into work that's already been booked in. I'm getting good at batting away all other small new jobs when that kind of thing happens. I've also built up a good roster of people to whom I can refer work I don't have time – or don't choose – to do, which means I can say "no", but, crucially, I can say, "But I can give you the name of a person who might be able to help" – and that makes me feel better.

I'm lucky enough to have a good set of regular clients. Over this year, I've become more choosy over who I add to my client list – clients I think will become regulars, the kind of work I enjoy doing, the financial aspects that make it worth doing – or with the less well-paid gigs, other factors such as enjoyment of the actual work. I'm looking at the areas of work I do and paying attention to what I like doing and what I don't enjoy so much. Some aspects of my work will diminish in importance as a result of this sifting. And I'm glad to have people, as I said, to refer new prospects on to if they come to me. For example, I don't think I'm going to take on many Master's coaching students this year. They are interesting to work with, but the unpredictability of the inevitably urgent work makes it hard to plan my week and be able to support the students. Luckily I know a great woman who is brilliant at taking students through their academic year, so off they go to help her build her business!

Autumnal balance

Autumn's a time of balance, isn't it? The year tipping towards the depths of winter. So there's going to be more balance here. Watching those autumn TV programmes with Matthew. Taking advantage of our new RSPB membership. Spending some time on my research project. Relaxing a bit now I'm half way through the financial year and know how I'm doing … It might not be back to school but it is back to a more balanced life, after a frankly odd summer.

October

Late September / early October saw – amazingly – my first bout of illness since I started being self-employed full time – although I admit that I did start off in December 2011 with a huge cold. That made me think – and write – about how to cope when you're ill, something that struck a chord with a lot of people. I do think I coped better this time than in December, which is all to the good.

But how can I be ill?

I have been asked before "What do you do if you're ill?" And then I WAS ill. Just a cold, but not very nice.

Obviously I don't get paid sick days, being self-employed (I have looked into this, with the help of ace accountant, Emily Coltman, from Freeagent and discovered that there is a similar thing to Statutory Sick Pay[16] that you can claim if you're self-employed). But the odd day or two just gets dealt with, basically. Anyway, here's how I cope with being ill and being self-employed.

Don't get ill

This is the main one. And it's not an admonition or a command: it should really read "I don't get ill". I had one cold in December 2011 and I've had one in September 2012. I honestly don't recall any in between. The reason must be that I don't work in an office any more. When I did, I was very careful about not coming in on the first day of an illness, and covering myself liberally with alcohol gel stuff before touching any handles, paperwork, etc. But not everybody was, and so while I didn't pass all of my bugs on, I certainly caught everything going (once I famously came back from a flu bug only to

---

[16] http://www.direct.gov.uk/en/MoneyTaxAndBenefits/BenefitsTaxCreditsAndOtherSupport/Illorinjured/DG_171891

catch a stomach bug, immediately). Add to that working on a campus full of students from all over the country, and world, or, before that, commuting on the Tube, and there you have it. Now I live in my little home office bubble, and there's only M to catch things from …

Don't work through it

When I was employed, if I felt unwell, I'd take the first day of illness off, stay in bed, and would recover much more quickly from the same bug than people who dragged themselves in. Last Christmas, I didn't do that. I had a fair bit of work on, but I'm sure I could have shuffled it around. But I didn't, and I was ill for longer than M, who had the same thing but was on holiday from work so not dragging himself anywhere. This time around, I took the first bad day pretty well off, just covering a small bit of work that needed doing urgently. M has dragged himself in with the same bug – and I'm getting over it more quickly.

Do work through it

Well, sometimes there are deadlines that have to be met. But I followed these rules this time, and aim to again:

* Just do what has to be done. No extras. No blog posts. No spreadsheets, just the work that must be done, then stop.
* Do it at the best time for me – after a decent lunch with some lucozade and painkillers in my case.
* Be kind to myself: it will take longer to do than normal, and that's fine.

This way, I've got what needs to be done, done, but have got enough rest, too.

Have back-up

This luckily hasn't applied this time, but back in the summer I had a somewhat spectacular reaction to an immunisation. Luckily for my clients, I had heroic Linda all set up – literally as a named back-up for some regulars, but available to have one-off work passed to her, too. There was no way I could work that day, so I let the regulars know to send work to her, and batted any enquiries over to her, too. No loss of professionalism there!

I hope this has helped clear up this mystery. If you're a self-employed person, now you have some pointers on how to cope when you're ill.

On getting slummocky aka doing your bank reconciliation

Slummocky is a great word, isn't it. I (re?)discovered it when reading Stella Gibbons' "Nightingale Wood". To be slummocky is to behave in an indolent or careless way, and a slummock is a slovenly person.

Now, of course, I'm NOT slovenly or careless or indolent. But I tell you what I have been doing, and that's letting the admin slide.

Not the invoices: no, of course not. I'm not actually stupid, and I would like my money to come in nice and regularly, thank you. And we all know that I run my accounts and do my tax return almost obscenely promptly every year.

But there are other things: deeper, darker, murkier things, which must be done when you're running your own business. Things like Bank Reconciliations. And like all admin or indeed everyday things, they are far better done regularly, in small doses, rather than in one great slummocky lump when you have started to panic about the huge bulk of them waiting to engulf you …

Bank reconciliations

The basic principle of the bank reconciliation is that you go through your accounts and your bank statement, and make sure they match up. A bit like the old-fashioned practice of balancing your cheque book – and we all do it to some extent, I'm sure, popping in to check the bank account online and make sure there are no unusual or incorrect transactions.

My friend Aly Mead at Silicon Bullet has written a great article on this subject; it's particularly good to read the article if you do your accounts in Sage or a system like that. I run my accounts via a spreadsheet (which I do keep scrupulously up to date) recording invoices raised and paid on one sheet and payments and charges on another.

Basically, I turn these two sheets into one long list of incomings and outgoings, listed by transaction date (i.e. the date the invoice was paid or payment made) (Spreadsheet A) and then I download a spreadsheet version of my bank statement (Spreadsheet B), and compare the two. I write the line number of the item on Spreadsheet A into a column on Spreadsheet B and vice versa, and then I rather satisfyingly colour them in green. In a basic version, the two look like this:

	A	B	C	D	E	F	G	H	I	J	K	L	M
1	ACCOUNTS							BANK ACCOUNT					
2	Date	Item	Money In	Money Ou	Running T	Bank Ac		Date	Item	Money In	Money Ou	Running T	Accounts
3	03/04/2012	Invoice 10	£12.00		£12.00	3		03/04/2012	Client A	£12.00		£12.00	3
4	04/04/2012	Mobile phone		£10.00	£2.00	5		04/04/2012	Client B	£40.00		£52.00	5
5	04/04/2012	Invoice 08	£40.00		£42.00	4		04/04/2012	Orange		£10.00	£42.00	4

Even though the entries aren't quite in the same order, I have matched them all up, and the running total is the same for both. I pop the accounts spreadsheet into the same order as the bank account spreadsheet at the end (I do this by sorting the spreadsheet by that column) and the two should match up.

Keeping up with the admin

If you do this every month, it's simple. It's like housework and ironing and all those other chores (actually, I never do ironing, but that's probably for another time). I only have between 20 and about 35 transactions per month. Which is fine when it's one or two months, not so great when it's … erm … nine.

And there are always little tweaky issues. I have missed putting a couple of payments in the right place on my main in/out spreadsheet, and forgot to record the info about a mystery payment, all resolved with the client a couple of months ago. I've also forgotten to pay myself back for membership of a website that I paid for using my own credit card. There is probably only one little issue per month, but when there are a few months to go through …

The other thing I've been a bit lax about is moving payments from other places. I have a PayPal account and a few regulars and one-off clients pay me by PayPal. I used to withdraw each payment immediately to my bank account, so it created one line on my bank statement which matched at most one in and one out on my accounts spreadsheet. But I've let these build up before withdrawing, which means I've got one line on my bank statement which matches five or six sets of incomings and fees on my accounts spreadsheet.

That will be changing, too.

Reforming my ways

I wrote this article to remind myself how hideous it is doing your bank reconciliation if you leave it too long. It's taken me a good few hours and given me a thumping headache. Don't be slummocky: little and often wins through!

November

November was another good month. It was coming up to the anniversary of my resignation from my library job – how amazing that that was a whole year ago! I had a good old think about motivation, and also, as I was having a slightly quieter few weeks for paid work, decided to run an experiment on my blog, and blogged each day for seven days about "What the well-dressed homeworker is wearing". This started off as a cheerful and light-hearted look at some frankly atrocious office wear (think bright pink tracksuit bottoms and moth-eaten fleeces) but turned into an interesting discussion on image and ability. I have extracted the main points of that set of blog posts into a single article, and highly recommend mixing up things on your blog by indulging in this sort of exercise once in a while. It got me plenty of hits and lots of comments!

First of all, let's talk about motivation – I learned some interesting things about myself and others when putting this article together.

How are you motivated?

How are people motivated, short term and long term? How do you motivate yourself and how does your boss motivate you? Is it all about the money …?

I started to think about this when I was playing a couple of Kinect games. Stay with me here, it is relevant!

The dancing game – at which I was pretty bad, being a) not very good at dancing or aerobics (not putting myself down here, just not good at moving fast in a coordinated manner. That's why I'm a runner) b) not used to this kind of thing. But the avatar dance trainer stayed really, really positive, even when it was clear I was doing badly. "Yo, you nailed that move," he shouted. Well, no, I didn't. If anything, the move nailed me.

Moving on ... I also tried out a fitness "game" – more of a set of workouts, but fun and interesting. The best thing about it was, though, that as well as getting the visual feedback on your movements that both games offered, in this one you got realistic feedback at the end. If you did well, you were told so. If you did badly, you got something along the lines of, "this wasn't quite what we wanted, but you can do better next time!" Just the acknowledgement that it wasn't the best go ever did motivate me a lot more.

So, realism and trustworthiness is obviously something that motivates me.

Short-term motivation and long-term motivation: chocolate or freedom?

I decided to undertake a scientific examination of this phenomenon. Well, no, I didn't: what I actually did was ask the question "what motivates you?" on Twitter, Facebook and LinkedIn. I wanted to see what real people who I actually knew said.

And the range of responses showed first of all that there is a difference between long-term and short-term motivators. The popular answer "chocolate" didn't mean (I think) that the respondent was motivated to do a good job, to achieve and excel, by a mountain of chocolate. But yes, a little sweet reward or some such is a great motivator to get something done. And tea, cakes and, indeed deadlines work in this way too.

Although ... deadlines ... is that more about having a job where you do have deadlines to hit? I would like to bet that the type of deadline you have in your job – if you enjoy it – is down to the motivators that work for you. Anyway, the long-term motivators are the interesting ones: recognition, praise, kindness make one group, which covers social or personally orientated motivators. Family, and even, from one respondent, cancer, show a deeply personal motivator which is probably about life achievements more than simple workplace ones. And then there is the set including independence, achievement and freedom (that's my one) which are more to do with the person themselves and their own interaction with their world (as opposed to interaction with people as such).

Do we see money in there? Well, it is mentioned, but it is not mentioned by anyone first.

Here's the scientific bit: Maslow's Hierarchy of Needs

This all comes down, in the end, to Maslow's Hierarchy of Needs or Maslow's Triangle. In an article written in 1943[17] (and also explained well in this Wikipedia article[18]), Abraham Maslow posited that we have a hierarchy of needs, and that the lower ones need to be fulfilled before the higher ones. So our basic key needs are the really basic ones – shelter, food, breathing, and next up are security of employment, body, health, property and family, among others. So our money need really disappears right at the bottom, or is maybe mixed into the one above. After these basic needs come love and belonging – family and friendship ties - then esteem, which includes self-esteem and the respect of others, and, at the top, self-actualisation: creativity, spontaneity, morality, problem-solving, etc.

You can see that most of the motivators my respondents talked about came from the upper levels of the triangle. Of course, when our health is threatened, we drop "down" a couple of levels, but then I suspect those who are motivated by their illness are actually reaching for esteem and self-actualisation, beating the illness and claiming their selves back.

---

[17] http://psychclassics.yorku.ca/Maslow/motivation.htm
[18] http://en.wikipedia.org/wiki/Maslow%27s_hierarchy_of_needs

Unpacking my motivators

So, when I "unpacked" my feelings towards my Kinect games (other consoles are available), I could see that I'm motivated by trust and truthfulness. When I was employed, I responded best to managers who were realistic but trusted me to get on with it , while speaking up if I was overwhelmed. Likewise, I wanted to trust them to give me the right work and leave me to it. I wasn't motivated by relentless optimism, and nor am I motivated personally by being shouted at, which is why I avoid the boot camp kind of exercise regime and hate being micro-managed. Now I work for myself, I can go up to the self-actualisation motivators and enjoy being creative and in control of sorting out my own problems. Freedom is a big one, too – I love having enough work to do to keep me busy but being able to do it when I want to, within my clients' deadlines, and being able to go to the gym (or stop and write a blog post) if I want to. Yes, I will get my head down and plough through a big project if I need to, but I know myself well enough to understand that that kind of rigidity is not healthy for me for more than a day or so at a time.

Count your blessings and Know Thyself

Of course, all those people who answered my question – and I – are lucky. We have enough money to live on and so our basic needs are covered, leading us to be able to be all esteemful and self-actualising. But when we're thinking about all of this, it's worth remembering that not everyone is so lucky, and giving something back if we can.

And: Know Thyself. Have a proper think about what motivates you. Look up Maslow and read his paper/a little more. Are you getting what motivates you out of your job, career or lifestyle? Are you in a position where you can change that? Is it worth having that chat with your boss about how you are really motivated? (although I wouldn't recommend being asked to be paid in chocolate coins …

In summary …

So it turns out

* we are not motivated by money … unless we really don't have any and we work our way up a hierarchy of levels to find more fulfilment
* short term motivators (chocolate! tea!) are different from long term motivators (family! freedom!) but both are useful
* it's good to sit down and have a think about what motivates you – it can be really useful in your career and life in general

What the well-dressed homeworker is wearing

This is a light-hearted exploration of what I and my fellow homeworkers were wearing, now that autumn was changing into winter, those home offices are getting chillier, and the layers of fleece are getting piled on.

I'm hired for my work and my brain, not my looks

I've always struggled with this corporate image thing, especially for women. Being expected to dress a certain way, to put on make-up, to look "right". I'm not talking about my right to be dirty or unkempt here, but to not dress up in what sometimes feels, to me, like drag. And I'm not criticising people who like to dress smartly, and especially not those people who dress very individually and interestingly – I'm talking about me and my resentment of the fact that I have had to present myself in a certain way in order to engender respect.

I'm lucky: I've not had many times in my life when I've had to dress up in office, suity attire. I do make an effort when I go to networking events or to do a presentation, but now I can pretty well choose what I want to wear. But I can remember times at trade shows where I've been openly criticised for wearing a dress and jacket, not a suit – "SO unusual", when it wasn't.

I'll openly admit that I've not had the courage to be different and stand out; I've always toed the line and slunk around in my suit and heels, trying to be invisible. I'm fairly introverted and quiet, and I don't really like to attract attention by my physical appearance. I do know businesswomen who have brightly coloured hair or unusual outfits and can manage to sail on past the criticism. I salute you!

Anyway, I've always maintained that it doesn't matter what people look like, but what they ARE like. Again, no to smelly and unkempt, but yes to pretty much anything else. And working invisibly like I do, on the other end of a wire(less), behind an email address, means that people probably don't know what I look like, and hopefully don't care. They hire me for my mind and my abilities.

Of course, human nature being what it is, I have been advised to, for example, have a photo on my About Me page of my professional website. And I have got one. And I am lucky enough to know Adam Yosef, who takes jolly good photos of me, looking like me. Cardi and scarf, a bit of make-up because, yes, I have got brainwashed into the whole image thing, and frankly it does make me look more awake these days, and we do have to present something of an image to the outside world, still, but it's me, I think. But I hope that my clients, and potential clients, have a look, OK, she's a human, a woman, about whatever age I look to be … and then concentrate on hiring the mind inside the outer casing.

This is a bit unfocused, but it's been interesting jotting my thoughts down. I know I'm the same person with the same gifts, mind and talents as when I was sitting at an office desk stuffed into a suit – but I'm a more comfortable and relaxed home for those gifts, mind and talents now.

The transition from office wear to home wear

I started off in a university library, without any real dress code but I changed from my student goth look to trousers and jumpers, having panicked I wouldn't fit in. Then the call centre was "anything goes, no one can see us!". At the Cable Company I recall skirts, tops and cardis, and I haven't changed much since then. At the Library Suppliers it was smart business wear at first - , so suits or suit trousers and tops - , but a new boss changed the code to business casual, so that was mainly an a-line or long skirt, top and cardi.

Then at the University Library again it was jeans or black polyester trousers, top and cardi, so I haven't really slipped far from there.

I did buy some "smarter" loose jersey trousers, tops and hoodies when I first started working from home a couple of days a week. This was to give me something special to wear for my new job, and to keep me out of manky house-cleaning / gardening outfits. I'm not sure that worked entirely, but I do wear them, and I will be sporting a full set tomorrow (today is a difficult mixture of personal training at the gym and helping out at the Social Media Surgery, so no room for jersey trousers there).

Now, timeless classics. Hmm. But what do you do with it all? I'm sorry – "timeless classics" are not timeless, they just last a few years longer than cheap fashion items. It's like when M tried on his black tie outfit, purchased while at University, ready for his brother's wedding a few years ago. There was, a cry of "The 80s called, they want their dinner jacket back" (and the trousers! Crikey! Post them back to MC Hammer!) and a swift trip to Moss Bros. I had various suits left over from the library supplier days, but they went off to the charity shop a white back. I have kept my black polyester trousers from the library years, but, again, haven't felt the need to indulge in their chilly static electricity since I've been working from home, and they will be trotting down the road soon enough. None of them suitable for the occasional client meeting and networking event I attend now. What do you do with all your office gear? Do you sit in your home study, shoulder pads at full cock, expensive watch glinting on your hand. Guys, do you wear Pink's shirts to do the gardening or under four jumpers?

My homeworking outfits for a week

Monday: Long-sleeved black cotton top from Primark, a bit baggy with extra-long sleeves coming down over my wrists; black skinny rib v-neck jumper. Black tights under black jeans, stripy socks I borrowed from my friend, Margaret, in 1994 – these initial layers are what a normal person wears in the daytime, because we walked to a distant Sainsbury's this morning.

Once home, I reverted to Homeworker specials – my beloved Sketchers Shape-Up sandals – they are loose fitting (well, adjustable) and rock, so I can move around when I'm sitting at my desk or stretching, and my ankles don't swell up any more; and a blue bodywarmer (OK, now it's called a gilet) which, amazingly for me, matches my shoes.

Tuesday: I admit that I did a bit of work before breakfast, and yes, I was transcribing in my pajamas, plus thick socks, plus a fleece. With the heater on. Well, it was 9.6 °C in the kitchen this morning! I went to meet a friend for a coffee in a nice warm cafe, so put on jeans, socks, a long-sleeved brown top and yesterday's black jumper, and now I've come up to the office to do blogging, book reviewing and a bit of light work (writing some articles for a website and a bit more transcription) and it is a little chilly, so I've added an extra, red, jumper on top of the other two tops. Nice and warm, but not too restricted.

Wednesday: pyjamas for the morning, and lovely warm grey and white hoodie that I've had since pre-M days, so we're talking 13 or so years. It's still cold, and a hood is good around the ears, although I might get a bit tangled up when I try to do some transcription!

Thursday: Gym kit for the morning; later jeans/top/cardi for popping out to help people at Social Media Surgery …

Friday: I started off the day in pajamas and fleece for a pre-breakfast transcribing session, transferred to yoga kit for the breakfast-to-yoga period, then moved up to my slightly less than shabby set of comfy clothes I bought to home work in back when I started doing this one day a week.…

Keeping up appearances

I'm quite happy to mooch around in pyjamas until lunchtime, and am often to be found in gym kit when it's yoga or gym day (which is most days). After getting up / getting back from the gym, especially in the winter, it's often straight into tracksuit bottoms and a fleece. But I do have limits …

> There are certain outfits which only go into the back garden and no further. This includes the famous Horror Pinks (very warm, fleecy-lined tracksuit bottoms in a lurid shade of hot pink; they only came in that colour, m'lud!) and Crocs with brightly coloured socks (actually, they go to the gym on yoga days, to ease speed of changing, but nowhere else).

> Other items will go to Sainsbury's and other basic shops, including the Post Office depot (a rare trip now*) – these include all tracksuit bottoms and gym outfits.

> I will wear gym outfits, i.e. yoga trousers and a gym top plus cardi to meet my friend Sian for a coffee on the High Street, but no further afield.

If I'm going into town, I will at least wear jeans/top/cardi or jumper (unless I'm doing the half marathon, in which case it's running leggings all the way, and a MEDAL on the way home).

When we were having work done on the house in the summer, I felt the need to shower and dress semi-properly (jeans and a top or gym kit) before Terry, our workman, got there - even though I know him , well, and I'm pretty sure he doesn't care what his customers look like.

While I don't mind what I look like opening the door to the postman or delivery men (one downside of working from home – the postman and all delivery people seem to share the knowledge that you're usually at home in the daytime, and deliver all your neighbours' parcels to you. But it keeps you close to your community, I suppose), I did shock one neighbour with my outfit (the bunches probably didn't help), so, when we were doing the Jubilee Party and I had people dropping by at all times, I tried to be more conventional-looking. That's all gone, now, though!

None of this stopped me finding myself on the front step of my house the other day in trackie bottoms, pink socks and Crocs, merrily on my way into town to meet Ali. It did send me back inside to change, though!

What do we wear when we do leave the house?

Today I want to talk about what we wear when we do get out of the house. The main thing I do out of the house is networking. Well, networking might be a fancy word for it: I'm quite well established now and not always out touting for new business, but I like to get out and about, chat with my peers, exchange ideas and find out how everyone's doing. I also love putting people together who could help each other. So, yes, networking.

For networking, I seem to have developed a bit of a uniform: skirt or trousers (usually my trusty black-jeans-that-don't-look-like-trousers), a jersey top, and a cardigan. Sometimes I even manage accessories: maybe a brooch, a ring and a watch! Wow!

An sometimes I climb into a skirt. Actually, even I, devotee of hoodies and fleece, like to get a bit dressed up now and then, and I do have some lovely things in my wardrobe which aren't really that suitable for my everyday activities of sitting at my desk or going to the gym. I love my bright skirts from H&M and don't really care that the A-line knee-length skirt is out of fashion. I have also admitted in the past that the Social Media Cafe,[19] run by the always exquisitely groomed Karen Strunks, is the only thing that makes me pluck my eyebrows and makes sure I can still get earrings in.

But looking through the photos from the Cafe (all taken by the lovely Adam Yosef[20] from Punk Zebra – if you ever need fab photos of yourself, go to him) I do notice a horrible reliance on a few cardigans that crop up time and time again. Do I need a new "capsule wardrobe" or is it not worth it for about 20 outings a year (I did do a presentation a while ago and really struggled to find something to wear to that. I was being a case study of someone who'd used social media for her marketing, I was among other small business people, and I could only find one outfit I thought was suitable.)

It's tricky, because it's not the suits of my formal office days, or the polyester trousers of my office girl days. I want to look a bit nicer, a bit more informal, maybe a tiny bit more up to date (although I've been ranting about the prevalence of smocks and puffed sleeves and detailing in current clothing for a couple of years now, none of them good for a short, high-waisted, small lady with broad shoulders!).

---

[19] http://birminghamsmc.com/
[20] http://www.twitter.com/AdamYosef

Do I need to go personal shopping or just trawl through TK Maxx? Has my trousers-cardi combo got stale? What should I do?

I had great fun writing my week of well-dressed homeworker posts. I've thought quite a lot about image, clothes, dressing up, etc. And I've learned a few things along the way, too!

> I am really comfy living the way I live and dressing the way I dress, and I'm comfortable with that, too.

> We all get cold and we should all wear more wool, silk and thermal undies.

> We all have pyjama days if we can get away with them.

> What's all this "getting away with it" mentality anyway – we're not hired for our looks, we're hired for our brains!

> Most of us like it best this way.

> We are still able to get out of the house, dressed in a conventional / tidy / decent manner that sometimes doesn't even involve any fleece!

Diary Entry 20 Nov: Give me a break! Well, yes, I will

The other month, I had an interesting time with busy-ness and quietness. I've been reflecting and mulling it over ever since. Yesterday, I wondered if I'd been overdoing it so I realised it was time to post this out into the world.

I had had quite a busy week, with one big project and lots of small to medium ones. It involved a lot of juggling, one late night, and a Thursday when I hammered through lots and lots of bits and bobs, to the possible consternation of onlookers. I had even had to turn down some work (new work, so as not to let down my current clients) and deflect some other tasks to my trusty emergency support proofreader, Linda (thanks, again, Linda). M had to cook dinner for an invisible girlfriend, only briefly seen foraging for food and tea …

But I am getting better at taking breaks, honestly. So when it got to the Friday and I'd got through the bits of work I had deadlines for, I then had a lovely long extended lunch break with a friend and her small daughter in the park, and a good long trip to the gym in the early evening, before stopping work for the day. At the weekend, I worked around the rest of my life, working on projects early and when M was out or wanted to watch TV. I even had a good long read in bed after breakfast on Saturday.

The article I wrote about presenteeism has helped me here: I realised that I posted a lot about working on social media, and was perhaps thinking too much about how much I work. I haven't scaled down what I do, but I've been aware of not taking too much on, and have obviously become better at scheduling things in and knowing how long jobs are likely to help. Keeping my reading journal on this blog has helped me to be more aware of making time for reading, and I make an effort to have time for friends and Matthew.

I feel like I'm getting it more right. I look after myself in the busy spells (and can usually predict them so I can work up to them and come to them healthy and relaxed) and don't panic in the quiet spells, taking that time to have some time out and enjoy myself.

I managed pretty well during the Olympics, watching most of the sport I wanted to see, and fitting my work around it. And I had a holiday in a place without reliable WiFi at the end of August, and survived, just about, having pre-warned my regular customers that I wouldn't be very available, and managing to relax about the whole thing.

As it comes up to a year since I left my library job and stopped trying to fit two jobs and the rest of everything into one life, I think I'm getting there with getting the balance. I've also been refining my customer base a bit.

December

December: month of sending your cards out late and not actually knowing which day Christmas falls on because you don't have to book time off work with an impatient boss who's juggling staff who all want to be off ... or maybe that's just me.

I was busy this month, with another new translation agency client coming on board, but I also had time for some reflection on the past year and on the future.

I finish up this section with an interview with myself. I have been running interviews with fellow small business owners since June 2011 with follow-ups to see how they're doing a year on. I didn't want to doom someone to a low audience the Saturday before Christmas, so interviewed myself (again usefully putting myself in my interviewees' shoes) in December 2011 and then did the follow-up between Christmas and New Year 2012. A good way to round off the year ... and this book (but watch out for some useful Appendices!).

The holy grail of passive income

Passive income really is the Holy Grail of many small business owners. Why? Because it's money you make without trying. Well, not really: you have to try initially, but once you've got your passive income stream going, it carries on flowing, whatever else you might be doing.

What is passive income?

Put simply, passive income is money you earn without doing anything for that particular chunk of money. Confused? Let's look at some examples.

You write a book and sell it through a bookshop or online as an e-book. People can buy it whenever and there is no demand on your time and effort once you've produced it and got it ready for sale.

You set up a referral link to Amazon on your website so that every time someone clicks through and buys something from Amazon, you get a percentage back.

You accept advertising on your website. You say OK to requests to place adverts (this is different from having a free blogging or website service that has adverts applied to it unless you pay the provider not to do that) and make the requisite part of your website available: someone else pays you a regular or one-off fee to host that advert.

Get the idea?

How do you start earning passive income?

Most people will do something connected with what they're doing already. Here are some examples drawn from Libro clients and people who've taken part in my small business chat feature:

> An author has created e-books and downloadables on how to publish an e-book, based on her experience publishing her first book
>
> A hypnotherapist has created CDs of hypnotherapy sessions which people can buy online
>
> A business advisor has franchised her business, so people pay her to run a similar business under the same brand name

You can see that in all of these cases it's not magic, effortless income: you have to put some kind of effort in first, be it negotiating with an advertiser or creating a resource or franchising model. But once it's done, all of these people can get on with their everyday life, knowing that their efforts will be bringing in income.

How am I developing a passive income stream?

For my normal run of income, I do some work, whether it's transcription, editing or proofreading, I charge my client for either the hours I spend or the minutes I transcribe or the words I edit, and I can't do any other similar work at the same time. One piece of work for one client, one chunk of income at a time. That's fine, but will only go to a certain point. So I have developed a couple of streams of passive income, and while they're only trickles at the moment, I hope to expand at least one of them in the future.

Referral fees. Having checked out their services and assured myself that they do a good job, I recommend self-publishing authors to use a print-on-demand publisher I know (this saves the authors having to pay upfront for millions of boxes of printed books that they have to sell themselves or, hopefully, getting ripped off). I am very clear when I recommend that I will be getting a small referral fee for this – so I'm not duping anyone into going for a service only because I will benefit. I haven't made much out of this so far, but it's there and something is better than nothing!

E-books. I published my first e-book, How I Conquered Cholesterol, a few months ago. It's selling small numbers steadily – OK, about 20 per month so far. It's made me around £40 in royalties so far – again, not much, but not nothing. It took me a few hours to write, so I haven't made back my initial investment in terms of those hours being worth money if I'd "sold" them to other projects – but I did this in down time, I didn't cancel any bookings to do so, and most importantly, I learned all about publishing e-books on Amazon from the process, which helps me understand what some of my clients need to go through.

And of course this e-book that you're reading now fits in nicely with part 2, too. And I am pretty sure that the larger market and the bigger group of friends and contacts I have in the small business world will help this one be more successful.

Remember to record your passive income in your accounts

Passive income doesn't come from an invoice. That doesn't mean that you can leave it off your accounts sheets, not pay tax on it or not record it at all! Here's what I do …

I keep paperwork for any passive income that comes in. Amazon sends me a statement when they send my royalties. These come straight into the bank account I registered with them. The publisher, at my request, sends me a statement of which people came to him and how much I am making for each, then transfers the money into my bank account.

I have a section on my accounts sheet for passive income, so that tots up and makes up part of my turnover and thus profit – and it can then be easily recorded in my bank reconciliation, too.

Diary Entry 13 Dec: Today is the first day of the second year of the rest of my life … and I'm thinking about tax

12 December 2011 was my last day in my old office. So today is semi-officially the first day of my second year of full self-employment, although I was still employed and paid by the University until 31 December, so there will be another celebration on 1 January. Happy days!

I paid my tax bill yesterday. I have been thinking about this subject recently, as there has been a furore over Starbucks, Amazon, etc., as well as various celebrities and people who are (in my opinion) rich enough already, using loopholes and legal means to squirrel away as much money for themselves as they can, ignoring what taxes are for, what they pay for, and the benefit they bring to the society among which and from which they make their money.

I'm not going to get overly political here. No, I'm not a fan of the present government, or of how they are distributing public funds, but the fact that there are any public funds to distribute in the first place is down in large part to people who do pay their tax.

I'm actually quite annoyed (especially in the year where I must pay double tax because of the payment on account system) that other companies operating in the UK are behaving like this, and giving businesses a bad name, too.

I have been checking on a few companies that I use recently to make sure I am making the most ethical choices I can (hooray for Eat and Lush!). And it struck me that I should make some sort of statement on my own position regarding tax. So I did, and I put it on my website.

Where now for Libro?

Can anyone see where Libro's going? I think I can, after a year of full-time self-employment.

It's hard when you become successful, as the advice that's given centres on growing your business by either taking on staff or franchising your business. But when your success and reputation rests on the work that you yourself do, this may not be appropriate.

At the moment, I have enough work to keep me busy, but not too busy, and to keep the money coming in

Rationalising your client base

This is a slightly tricky subject, as it's all about optimising income (which sounds all very corporate and businessy and Not Very Nice, but has to be done if you're going to actually succeed and support yourself) and, for me, maintaining the interest and enjoyment of doing the actual work. I think I've balanced this quite well at the moment. I have a mix of:

> Localisation work and work with translators - this is my most valuable skill in terms of the fees I can charge for the work. It can range from interesting to not-so-interesting, but the clients I'm working with are really nice and I know them quite well now, and they usually book me in advance and give me decent deadlines that I can cope with.
>
> Other general editing and writing work, usually for clients I've had for a number of years now. Good, solid work that I am familiar with and even if I don't get booked that far in advance, I usually have a good understanding of the rhythms of their work.
>
> Student work - I usually have a PhD in the pipeline, and still have a couple of on-going student clients, although I have not gone out to take lots of people through their Master's course this year, as I did last year, tending to pass such clients on to a recommended colleague. I like the return to academic writing I get here, and the intellectual challenge, as well as learning in depth about new topics.
>
> Music journalists. This is my fun work. I give them special rates because they're usually freelancers too, so the return per hour is well down on the first or even the second category. But I love music and these are so interesting, the clients are lovely, and even though they often can't book me in advance and can send me very, very rush jobs, I really enjoy the work and can usually fit them into my schedule. The rates I get here are subsidised by the more lucrative jobs in the first category.

I think it's SO important not to lose touch with what I enjoy doing. I can offer cheaper rates to my journalists because my skills in other areas command a higher standard rate that subsidises them. It's a bit like when I was a busker - I could have played "Moon River" and "Streets of London" over and over again and made more money, but for my sanity, I kept a variety of tunes in my repertoire.

Where now - business sustainability

So I have my client base pretty well established and it's sustainable, keeping on with regulars, eggs in quite a few baskets so losing one won't wreck my business, and adding the odd new one, but sensibly.

I didn't want to just turn work down that I can't take on myself, and, as I've mentioned, it is not suitable for me, personally, to take on staff to do the additional work. So these past few months, I've gathered together lists of trusted people who do the various things that I do, and so when someone comes to me with some work I can't fit in - or when a regular needs me but I have a holiday booked - I can pass them on to a trusted and recommended person who I know will do a good job for them. That satisfies my basic need to be helpful and kind and not leave people in the lurch.

How are you growing your business? What path are you choosing? Why not read this book through in a year's time and see how different you're feeling then?

Rounding off the year: an interview with myself

I published an interview with myself on Christmas Eve 2011, just after my adventures in full-time self-employment began. It was part of my Small Business Chat series, and what I said there was a short version of what I say in this book, so I'm not going to bore you with that.

When I asked myself where I planned to be in a year's time, I answered, "**Well, I'll have been full-time with Libro for a year. Hopefully I'll be earning enough to support myself, I'll have taken a holiday or two, and have a good solid roster of regular clients to keep me going**". Let's see how I'm doing ...

Are you where you thought you'd be when you looked forward a year ago?

Yes! I have been full-time for a year, I'm earning more than enough to support myself - it's so nice to be able to have lunch out when I want to, or treat myself to some nice pampery toiletries in the sales, and to be able to buy my friends nice birthday and Christmas presents. I have had one holiday and some time off, I've got better at scheduling in time off, and I do indeed have a solid roster of regular clients to keep me going - I've added one or two per month this year.

What has changed and what has stayed the same?

The main thing is having only one job - much easier. I have been able to spend more time with my friends and with Matthew. I have stopped working with Master's students through their course, as I discovered this was quite draining and gave rise to lots of urgent panicky work for people's deadlines (I've been able to recommend such prospects over to a friend who specialises in academic work and is great at working with students). I've published one e-book and I'm about to publish another, so I should have some sort of passive income stream soon. What's stayed the same? I'm enjoying my work still (hooray!) and enjoying working with clients around the world. And, apart from a brief flurry around the beginning of the year and then September, when I presented my paper at the Iris Murdoch conference, I haven't finished writing up my research project, although I have finished the questionnaire gathering side of it.

What have you learned? What do you wish you'd known a year ago?

I've learned to be better at stopping work to have the evening off, to not panic when the work goes quiet, and how to work on my own, I suppose. I wish I'd formulated some of my tips for homeworkers sooner so I could make sure I was looking after myself. I also wish I'd found some back-up people earlier, so I can be ill or busy without worry.

Any more hints and tips for people?

If you're thinking about jumping ship from your full- or part-time day job, and you've got the money saved up to support yourself for a few months ... go for it!

And ... where do you see yourself and your business in a(nother) year's time?

I've got some personal plans bubbling away, and I'd like to be training for a marathon in the next year or two. Business-wise, I would like it to be pretty well as it is now - a good roster of interesting regular clients keeping me busy and keeping my income steady.

April 2013

A mature business

I meant to publish this book in January 2013. But various bits and pieces (not least getting it edited by a proper editor who did a fantastic job for me) meant that it got a bit delayed. However, this has given me the opportunity to look back on my first year and write this never before published report from four months on …

I now consider Libro to be a mature business. Why do I think this?

I earn a decent wage, more than I've ever earned before, and that means I can have nice things and go on holiday.

I have a good work-life balance. I rarely work in the evenings now, I have time at the weekends for friends, family and hobbies, and I have a good balance of work, personal projects and fitness in the daytime

I have a good roster of regular clients who I know well and with whom I have a mutual understanding. Some of these have been with me for years; the newer ones have been selected carefully to fit in with my availability and the work I prefer to do.

I have a great set of colleagues in editing and the other areas I work in, and in the small business world at large. We get together, laugh and moan, support each other – and I'm helping at least two other editors make the leap into full-time self-employment that supports them financially and psychologically.

I am giving back. I haven't turned into a raving Tory. I won't even mind if I pay top-rate tax. I help and support others, I give to charity, I publish information for free on my website to help other people.

I get bored! No longer is everything thrilling and new, romantic, something I live and breathe. I have distance, sometimes I do trudge up the stairs to the office unwillingly (not often though!). It's my job, and it supports my lifestyle.

I wasn't a natural entrepreneur. I didn't take risks. I'm earning well, I'm happy and I'm fulfilled. I've changed as a person – I'm far more confident and calm (and fitter!). If I can do it, as I turned 40, so can you!

Conclusion

So, that's it – a year in the life of a full-time self-employed editor, proofreader, localiser and transcriber. I hope you've enjoyed reading about my experiences, and maybe it's taught you a thing or two, or given you some ideas. Read on to the Appendices for more on how to decide whether to go self-employed, how exactly to do it, and some other useful hints and tips.

If you have enjoyed this book and/or found it useful, PLEASE submit a review to Amazon. I'm one, self-published, person in a sea of other writers. The only way people can judge whether this is any good is by reading reviews. So please consider sharing what you thought about the book on Amazon, your blog, Facebook or Twitter.

If you have any feedback that you'd like to give me, please do get in touch – I'd be delighted to hear from you.

And if you're planning to take the plunge and work for yourself – good luck! You can do it!

Liz Broomfield

April 2013

liz@libroediting.com

Twitter: www.twitter.com/lyzzybee_libro

Facebook: www.facebook.com/libroediting

Libro website and blog for Word and language tips and hints, small business interviews and the serious stuff: www.libroediting.com

Libro full time blog for more on my journey to self-employment plus book reviews and other fun stuff: www.librofulltime.wordpress.com

Appendix 1: So you want to be a freelancer?

Fancy going into freelancing? Here's what you need to think about before you go for it.

Before you start

There are quite a few things it's worth thinking about before you launch yourself into a freelance career. Here are some of the main ones:

Do I have useful skills that people are prepared to pay for? If you're already doing something in your daily work life that you would like to do on your own, then yes, you may well have (but see below warnings about doing the same thing for an employer and yourself). If you've just got a general idea about going into business for yourself, think about skills you have developed as part of your job or a hobby. I had done a fair bit of editing and writing in various jobs, but it didn't strike me how many different things I could offer until I was running the business. I could have offered more from the very beginning.

Is there a market for my particular skills, and will I be able to access it? If you're experienced in a particular area, do you have contacts who will help you find freelance work? Contacts are the key. Are there companies who might take a sample, for example shops which might stock your knitted widgets or people who might share a stand at a craft fair? Think about specialist skills you might have – for example, I have experience working for the UK office of an American company, so I'm able to offer localisation services changing US into UK English.

Can I work from home on my own? Most freelance jobs do involve a fair bit of working alone. Even a photographer or someone who sells through a market stall will need to spend a fair amount of marketing and admin time alone. Are you good at motivating yourself? If you need people around you – well, co-working spaces can be very useful, but there is still a fair bit of sitting in your house pondering, doing admin, and getting on with work.

How will this affect the rest of my life? This is ever so important if you're thinking of starting your own business while still working. As I said at the beginning, that's how I've done it, and there have been times when I've had so much of my own work that I've had to put off friends, tell my partner he can only spend time with me if he sits in the chair in my study (silently!) and I've pretty much given up reading for pleasure. Can your social and family life take this? Make sure you have your partner and/or family's support.

Early days

Once you've answered these questions and decided to set up on your own, I advise doing the following:

Getting yourself **online**: it's wise to get hold of a domain name right away (so that the URL of your website will be http://www.YourCompanyName.com and not http://www.YourCompanyName.wordpress.com for example), and set up a web page and email addresses using it. It is generally agreed that you look more professional if you do this. And the more professional you appear to be, the more business you will attract.

If you're in the UK, go on the **HMRC** course "Becoming self-employed" (find information in your local library or on the HMRC website). This is my number one recommendation to people starting a business. The course leader will tell you what records to keep so you can do important things like your tax return, and they tell you all about what to do, what funding and special tax breaks you can get, etc. If you're not in the UK, there will be a similar organisation linked to the government tax office which should offer advice and information.

Again, in the UK, **register your business** with HMRC – you have to do this within a certain period after you start working and being paid for it. Have a look on their website or give them a ring. Their staff have always been very friendly and helpful when I've called them. If you're outside the UK, there will be a similar body with which you will need to register.

UK again – register for a **Certificate of Small Earnings Exception** – this allows you to earn a certain amount before paying National Insurance and tax. Not in the UK? Check out support for start-ups – there's lots out there.

Get **business cards** – at first you can use somewhere inexpensive like Vistaprint but it's important to have something to give out to potential clients and people who might recommend you. Don't go for gimmicks, just business cards will do at the start.

Be careful if you want to do as your own business something that you are already doing in your **day job**. You might be about to be made redundant. If so – use those skills. If you're going to do it part-time while still working in that area, make sure your employer is OK with that and check your contract – ditto if you leave to set up on your own. Better safe than sorry – and you will get found out.

Appendix 2: How to go about being self-employed

Right, so once you've gone through the questions I posed in Appendix 1 and decided that you are suited to freelance work, and you've been on the initial courses that I recommended, it's time to set up good, reliable working practices right from the start. These are some things I've found handy:

• **Prioritise.** This is key. Make sure you have time for work, yourself and other people. If you work all hours, you'll run yourself into the ground. That won't do anyone any good. And if you are likely to end up doing lots of little projects …

• **Organise**. I set up a Gantt chart on a spreadsheet – clients down the side, dates along the top, and I colour-block in dates that projects are booked in for, changing the colour as they arrive, when I've invoiced, when they've paid. It's a really good way to see what you've got on and whether you can fit in that extra client project.

• Set up **terms and conditions**. I have standard email text that I sent out when I'm quoting for a job, stating when I will ask for payment, how they can pay, what I'm doing, etc. For larger ongoing clients, I set up an agreement in a Word document and make sure we've both agreed to it. It's better to know how you're going to end things or deal with conflicts before it comes to the crunch.

• **Invoice**. Make sure you invoice clients as soon as you've done the job. Or before, if you work that way round. If you arrange to invoice people for several projects at the end of the month, do it. There's software you can buy, or you can just set up a Word template. Then make sure you check and record their payment. That's where the Gantt chart comes in handy. Not in green – they haven't paid and it might be time to chase up.

- **Use tools.** Make sure you have up to date and legitimate versions of the software you need – Word, etc. If you will be working with any kind of software, whether to read knitting patterns or invent widgets, there are often free downloads available, or trial copies (make sure you buy or delete once the trial is up. Not only are you doing the right thing legally, but paying will often mean access to updates, support and more professional results. You may also be supporting other small businesses who market this software. Authors' tool, Scrivener, only had money to develop their PC version because of the Mac users who bought it!

- **Work for your clients, not yourself.** Some of my clients, like students and translators, need me to show all the changes in Track Changes so they make the decision on what to change and I'm not writing their work for them. Other clients just want me to go in, rewrite and send it back to them. Offer your clients choices, but be prepared to make recommendations based on what similar people have requested, too.

- Be **flexible and open**. I started off as an editor and proofreader. But as clients asked me to do more things, I added in writing, transcription, copy-typing and localising to my portfolio. All things I could actually do already! More income streams, more work! Have a think about what you can offer outside of your core products. If you knit toys, why not run a class or knit some weird shapes for adults. That came out a bit funny, but you know what I mean!

- **Network.** Both among your peers (in the business and other freelancers who work from home) and among other businesspeople in your area. Twitter and Facebook are useful for finding out what's going on. It gets you out of the house and meeting people. LinkedIn offers business networking online – join the groups and get chatting.

- **Outsource**. Know when you need help. If something is going to take you longer and cost more in terms of work you would have to drop or postpone while you're doing a task, outsource. Freelance journalist? Get someone else to transcribe your tapes. Not good at sums? Get a bookkeeper or accountant in to control your records. It's also useful to know people in the same line of business as you to whom you can pass work in an emergency.

I hope you find these handy hints useful. I've grown in confidence and developed my skills and, not a natural entrepreneur, have built a successful and flourishing business!

Appendix 3: A Homeworker's Resolutions

1. I will get out of the house every day, in daylight if humanly possible.

2. I will speak to someone other than myself and my partner / housemate / spouse / parent / child / sibling [delete as applicable: I want to be inclusive here!] every day, even if it's just an email conversation (but I'll try to make it a face-to-face conversation).

3. On at least 4 out of 5 weekdays I will eat a proper lunch. By a "proper lunch" I mean something that has more than one food group, including fruit and/or vegetables, and is not constituted primarily of cereal

4. This lunch will be consumed by 2 p.m. every day, at the absolute latest. It's not necessarily BAD to have lunch late – I have my breakfast later now, so that I can have a chat with M first thing, so I'm not fainting by this point, but it is important to have regular anchors when you're alone all day, and I think this one is important.

5. I will leave the phone alone at mealtimes. I've been REALLY bad at this one. All those little email messages binging into my phone with that tempting noise. And I do have a lot of regular clients who need work doing at short notice. But, honestly, in the time it takes to consume a meal, is anything so urgent going to happen that it would really matter if I put the phone to one side? Do I need to be twisting round to grab my phone, only to find it's spam or bacon*? I started to try this at lunch and extended it to dinner, too. Fair enough, I will have the phone within reach in the evening, and it's by my bedside as I find it comforting to just check if something's come in without getting out of bed first thing. But mealtimes are now sacred.

*bacon is stuff you've signed up for but then feels almost like it's spam when you receive it – newsletters and updates, that kind of thing

6. I will wash up and reuse my mug. I will not use all of the mugs in the house in one or two days

7. I will go to an event outside the house at least once a week: networking, meeting a fellow freelancer friend for lunch etc. This does not include social occasions with friends or aforementioned partner/housemate/whatever

8. I will keep up with my friends' doings

9. I will endeavour to stop work at 7 in the evening, and at midday at the weekends (unless I have urgent projects to complete). Your rule may be different: having a rule is what's important.

10. I will spend more time with my aforementioned partner/spouse/whatever.

11. I will spend at least a little time every day doing something I love (that's not my job, which I may well love too). I'm getting better at this one – hooray! In my case, this thing that I love is reading. I was missing reading: I've always been a big reader and love reading and reviewing what I've read. I set up a nice new home for my book reviews, which has helped with this. And I've taken to grabbing a book when I'm on the way to the gym once a week, and reading on the exercise bike (yes, I still have a good, hard workout!). I'm happier as a result, and less panicky about the size of my Mount To Be Read. Even if you love your job, do a little different thing, whether it's watching the telly, reading a magazine, or having a bath. If it's a special thing you can do every day, like reading, so much the better!

Appendix 4: Top Ten Tips for Working with Clients

As a freelancer, I've spent three years (so far) learning how to deal with lots of different clients. I hope that these tips will help you get the most out of the relationship. If you work with freelancers, you might find the next article useful, too.

1. Communicate

This is the **top tip**, and comes into many of the other sections. Be clear about **what you do, how much it costs, and when you can do it**. Communicate the way in which you work to your client up front. Keep on top of the project and let them know how it's going. Tell them what to expect, then **fulfil that expectation** and communicate that you have done so.

2. Manage expectations

It's always best, in my opinion, to **promise low and deliver high**. I always add a little time when I'm offering a deadline, and almost always exceed expectations that way. If you are going to miss a deadline, let the client know – this only usually happens when it's the client who sets the deadline. I've only missed one deadline, by half an hour – but there was good reason for it, and I let my client know in advance.

If you're undertaking a project for someone and they've not used a freelancer before, explain the process and what they can expect from it. If you need to tell clients about your terms and conditions, send those along with your initial quotation. If an urgent job will cost more, tell the client in advance.

If you can't offer the service you would want to offer, **a "no" said honestly and in good faith is better than a "yes" that isn't meant**. Your client will respect you more for it.

3. Keep to deadlines

If you promise to return a piece of work to a client by a particular date and time, do your utmost to do this. Work all night if you have set an unrealistic deadline (and learn from that!). When I started freelancing, I found that freelancers have a very bad reputation around this issue. Ignoring deadlines makes you look arrogant at best, incompetent at worst. It's not hard to **plan ahead**, and it's not hard to say no (eventually).

This also applies to **invoicing**. If I've arranged to invoice the client directly after finishing the work, I do so. If they are on a monthly invoice in arrears, they are sent their invoice at the end of the month. If this is a bit much, it's something you can easily automate or outsource.

4. Treat your client as a human being

Even if your client is a huge faceless entity, you will be dealing with a **person** from that organisation. Remember that they're a human being, with other concerns than you and the project you're both working on. They may be trapped between you and their own boss or client (I work for several freelance journalists and translation agencies, for example) and may have other pressures. If they're a student or a new member of staff, they may be unsure as to how to work with you!

5. Inform your client about your availability

If you've got a holiday booked, you don't work on weekends, or you stop at 9pm at the latest, **let your clients know**. When I book a holiday, I send an email to my main regular clients a few months before, remind the biggest ones a month before, put a note in my signature then set up an auto reply on my email. Out of courtesy, I do communicate with them by email when I'm away, but only to remind them I am away!

6. Have backup

For my major clients, I have colleagues who do the same line of work as me and can pick up work if I'm unwell or on holiday, or very busy with a pre-booked job. I also have a list of people I can **refer** clients on to if I can't book them in myself.

7. Respect your clients

Professionally and personally. You're the expert in what you do, but they're the expert in what they do. Treat them as you would expect them to treat you. Be as robust as you need to be, but **always be courteous**.

If you feel the need to let off steam about a tricky client or project, please do it **privately**! I have a little group of fellow editors of whom I can ask questions and with whom I share good and bad days – and sometimes people do make us a bit cross, but we just don't broadcast this in public. It's not very professional, and it can reflect on you very badly.

You may have specific points with this according to the industry you're in. I personally avoid pointing out horrible grammar and spelling mistakes on signs and menus in public. Amusing as I find these, a lot of my clients are using English as a second or third language, have issues with their English skills, or are just not very confident, and the last thing I would want to do would be to be seen to be mocking less-than-perfect English.

8. Work with your client's working methods

You have to be **flexible** if you're going to be good at freelancing for different clients. They all have different requirements and ways of working. In my case this can go from noting which transcription clients need a time stamp every 5 minutes and which need it every 10 minutes, to communicating via email, the phone or a face-to-face meeting - whatever the client prefers.

I do impose my own working methods on them to an extent, for example encouraging them to use comments and Track Changes to comment on texts I've produced for them. But if they choose not to do that, I'll fit with how they want to work.

9. Share the joy

I have a list of people who do what I do who I will **recommend** to any clients I can't fit in. I don't consider them as competitors – yes, we're in the same line of business, but everyone gets work they can't do for whatever reason, and I'd rather have a known person I can send things to, knowing they are likely to do a decent job. This saves clients (particularly students) from getting ripped off, and I think it presents a professional attitude to the prospective client, too.

10. Say thank you

I try to say **thank you** whenever a client pays me. I also thank them for being particularly good clients – the student who doesn't automatically "accept all changes" but asks me questions about their English, the writer who's produced an interesting book … and if a client has a product or service I think is particularly good, I'll pop a link on my links page here and tell people about their book, service or product. It doesn't cost anything to say thank you, after all, and it gives your client a great final impression of you!

Appendix 5: Top Ten Tips for Working with Freelancers

As a freelancer, I come across all sorts of clients and all sorts of behaviour. If you outsource work to freelancers yourself, whether you're a **tiny company** outsourcing to an accountant and a copywriter or part of a **huge tech company** with hundreds of freelance programmers on your books, these tips will help you get the most out of the relationship. And isn't it funny how similar they are to my top ten tips for freelancers …!

1. Communicate

This is tip number one, and feeds into so many others of the top ten. Be **clear** in your initial communications. Express your requirements clearly. If anything **changes**: the project, the deadline, the date you can deliver the project to them, your expectations – tell your freelancer. They're not a mind reader: you need to tell them.

2. Manage expectations

If you commission a chatty, friendly blog post and you get a piece of corporate spin, did you really express what it was that you wanted? Again, freelancers are not mind-readers. A good writer can write in whatever style you want – but they do need guidance. Like a computer, a freelancer will **absorb your instructions and produce output to the brief given**.

A good freelancer will check what you want, and in some cases will send you over a questionnaire to fill in or have a chat with you over the phone. Use this opportunity.

3. Keep to deadlines

If you **promise** to deliver a project specification, a document, a set of keys, whatever, to your freelancer, on a particular day at a particular time, then either **keep to that agreement** or, if you can't, **let them know** as far in advance as you possibly can. Everyone has sudden last-minute issues and no one minds that, but freelancers do mind booking in a job, possibly turning away other clients because that time is booked, then no work arriving.

Similarly, if your **end deadline changes**, keep your freelancer informed, give them the chance to adjust their schedule, and understand if they can't. Perhaps you're a journalist and your editor changes when they need that interview write-up – let your transcriber know as soon as possible and show willing to pay an urgent fee or make the deadline as flexible as possible.

This applies to **payments**, too. Make your company's payment schedule clear **in advance** (no – "oh, yes, it's a 60 day payment schedule; didn't I tell you?" please) and make sure you pay on time or let the freelancer know if you can't.

4. Treat your freelancer as a human being

This seems to apply especially in office-type services, such as editing and virtual secretarial services. Several colleagues have commented privately that they feel like some of their clients think of them as a piece of office machinery, like a printer or network cable, and are then scandalised when real life – an emergency, a holiday – intervenes. **Just because you can't see your freelancer doesn't mean they don't have a face and a life**! (I'm lucky, pretty well all of my clients treat me well and even let me go on holiday occasionally!)

5. Inform your freelancer about your availability

If you're **going on holiday**, or you don't work Mondays, let the person you've commissioned know. They might have a question and not be able to get in touch with you. Leading on to …

6. Have backup

Is there someone else in your organisation who could **pick up the reins** with your freelancer(s) if you were to go off sick or go on holiday? I've had situations where my contact at a client's office has gone out sick, and no one's been told about the projects I'm working on or when I should be paid.

7. Respect your freelancer

Professionally and personally. They're the expert in what they do, just like you're the expert in what you do. You've hired them to do a job, so **let them do that job**. If you feel you know how to do whatever you're asking them to do, remember that it might be a part of your job, but it's their speciality. Of course it's fine to ask questions, but if you've chosen right, from a recommendation or by checking out the freelancer's references and experience, let them get on with their job.

Having said that, I'm pretty sure I've typed some terrible mis-hearings into transcriptions I've done for clients, but I've never (thankfully) seen them **laughing about it in public**. Don't make assumptions about their private life – it's polite to ask if they mind working through the weekend on your project, even if they've done so before. I don't mind working odd hours for my clients, as I make up for it with long lunch breaks with gym sessions and a sit in the garden, but I appreciate it when they realise that I have a life, too!

8. Work with your freelancer's working methods

Although a good freelancer will **adapt the way they work** to suit you to a certain extent, there are times when you need to **fit in with how they work**. For example, if a client needs to comment on a text I've produced for them, I request them to do so in Track Changes, rather than colouring in bits of text and writing comments in the text. It's easier for me to work my way through the comments, saving the client time and money if they are on an hourly rate, and I will always take a moment to explain how to do it.

9. Share the joy

If someone does a good job for you, **offer them a reference or testimonial**. Tell other people about their services. I get most of my work through recommendations, and it's a great way for clients to get freelancers they know will be good, and freelancers to get clients who are likely to go with them because their friend or colleague has recommended them.

A freelancer who knows you've recommended them on to your friends and colleagues will be more loyal to you. They'll want to do a good job for you, so you recommend them again!

10. Say thank you

On the day I wrote this post, I'd been up since 5.30 am to turn around a very urgent project for a client. What really did make that worthwhile? The client coming back to me to say a big thank you. It really does matter; it doesn't take a moment, and it cheers everyone up.

Appendix 6: Setting Goals

Why set goals?

This section is about setting goals, primarily in business, but of course this can be used in the rest of your life, too. Why set goals? It gives us something to aim for, and, if done properly, should give us a way of measuring our progress towards our goal, too. Goals and the progress towards them can help us make big life changes; it was through measuring my progress against a specific set of goals that I was able to leave my part-time job and start running Libro full time, and I'm not the only person to achieve a big life change like that.

Setting sensible goals

There's lots of talk, especially in a business context, of setting SMART goals (Specific, Measurable, Achievable, Realistic and Timely). But actually, I think you can get away with just setting sensible goals.

The end target should be something you actually want, whether it's working at your business full time, growing your hair for your wedding or running a marathon. This will probably be inspired by what motivates you, something that I wrote about in November. In my case, I wanted to work full time because I wanted the flexibility to run my life how I wanted to, and the free time to spend reading and with my friends. These motivators meant I really wanted to do it. You can't set goals half-heartedly, because you will not work towards them if you do. And they can't be other people's goals, either. Think how much more fun and easier it is to learn a language so you can order a beer on holiday, rather than toiling away for a GCSE at school.

The method to achieve this target should involve a specific set of activities that are measurable along the way. For me, I had to be earning a certain amount per month in order to be able to support myself. If you're training for a marathon, you need to be able to run a certain distance by a certain time. If you want a particular wedding hairstyle, you need to go to the hairdresser for a trim to keep it looking good and know how long your hair needs to be for the special style.

Ideally, you should be able to chart how you're doing and measure it against how you should be doing. So you might take photographs of your hair, I had spreadsheets and graphs to tell me how I was doing against my financial targets, and a runner will tick off training sessions and achievements as they go.

Measuring your progress

It is **vital** to measure your progress as you go along. In my case, last year I knew how much I needed to be earning per month to support myself. I keep a list of incoming and outgoing money, so I copied my income over onto a new sheet of my spreadsheet, so I knew what had come in that month. I then compared that to what I needed to be earning per month to support myself. At first, I compared it to how much money I needed to replace the money lost by going part time, so I had a set of columns and a graph – a graph does a good job of showing you where you stand – that told me where I was against a monthly target and also a cumulative target (that meant that if I earned less one month and more the next, they averaged out and meant I was still hitting my annual target).

Although it sounds complicated, it was easy to do in practice, and it showed me that I hit the targets for replacing my lost income quite quickly, and began to hit and beat the target income for supporting myself. That's when I knew it was time to leave and strike out on my own.

Set challenging targets

I like to have an easy, middling and hard target. I'll always achieve something, but I strongly believe that having something challenging to go for has meant that I have achieved more. Last year I measured my income against replacing my lost income from 2 and 3 days a week and against the lowest amount I needed to support myself. Building up through the year, I only missed that top target by £100 – and I really wasn't expecting that. So this year I have that as my lowest target, my old full-time wages as my middling one, and an amount I haven't earned since I lived in London as my hard target. Don't get excited: it's not a fortune and I'm not going to turn into a millionaire. But by setting that high target, I'm giving myself something to aim for.

Affirmations and speaking out loud

Apart from the hard target that pushed me forward, I am convinced that what helped me achieve was vocalising and affirming. Otherwise known as telling people what I was doing. Part way through 2011 – and remember that I didn't actually decide to leave my part-time job until November – I started telling people, "I am aiming to go full time with the business some time in early 2012," or "by a year from now I will be full time with Libro." These weren't affirmations in the traditional, chanting in front of the mirror or writing them on a bit of paper sense, but speaking my targets out loud did help me to achieve them.

I hope this has been helpful. I try to talk about specific examples of what I've done, to show that it is possible – no high-falutin' promises of millions! Maybe you'd like to share the goals you've set and how you set them. What helped you – or is helping you – to achieve them? And do let me know if this has inspired you to set some sensible goals yourself. That's the first step to speaking it out loud!

Appendix 7: Resource guide

Here are some resources you might find useful as a first-time freelancer. Some are specific to editing, some are specific to women, all will be useful to someone!

Bernadette Jones – "The No-Nonsense Women's Guide to Setting up a Business" – tells it how it is, with lots of support for women business owners

Emma Jones – Enterprise Nation – support, events, books and more for the budding business owner www.enterprisenation.com

Adam Yosef – Punk Zebra – if you need film or photography for your business and you're in the Midlands, Adam's the person I trust to take great pics of me www.punkzebra.com

Louise Harnby – "Business Planning for Editorial Freelancers" – an e-guide on specific information for the editorial profession

Thank you for reading right to the end! Do review, share and talk about this book, and get in touch at liz@libroediting.com if you want to ask me anything!